PURE & SPECIAL

First published in 2014 by

INTERLINK BOOKS
An imprint of Interlink Publishing Group, Inc.
46 Crosby Street
Northampton, Massachusetts 01060
www.interlinkbooks.com

Published simultaneously in India by Roli Books,
New Delhi

Library of Congress Cataloging-in-Publication
Data available
ISBN 978-1-56656-959-0

Publisher: Michel S. Moushabeck
Editor: Neeta Datta
American edition editor: Leyla Moushabeck
Book design: Sneha Pamneja
Photography: Sanjay Ramchandran
Production: Shaji Sahadevan, Naresh Nigam
Proofreading: Jennifer M. Staltare
Cover design: Julian Ramirez

Printed and bound in Star Standard, Singapore

10 9 8 7 6 5 4 3 2 1

To request our complete 48-page, full-color
catalog, please call us toll free at 1-800-238-
LINK, visit our website at www.interlinkbooks.
com, or e-mail: info@interlinkbooks.com

PURE & SPECIAL
GOURMET INDIAN VEGETARIAN CUISINE

VIDHU MITTAL

Photographs
SANJAY RAMCHANDRAN

Interlink Books

An imprint of Interlink Publishing Group, Inc
Northampton, Massachusetts

CONTENTS

ACKNOWLEDGMENTS

This book has been a team effort and would not have been possible without the wonderful group of professionals, friends, and well-wishers who've worked patiently and tirelessly to help turn my dream into reality.

Abhishek Poddar: For his tireless encouragement and for being able to articulate so perfectly, through his creativity and design aesthetic, my vision for this book.

Jagadish Babu: For his ability to painstakingly sort hundreds of photographs and reams of content into a logical order that finally became the book.

Sanjay Ramchandran: His passion for food and endless patience brought out the true essence of each recipe through exquisite photographs.

Sonya Balasubramanyam: For her remarkable attention to detail and for helping me meticulously put together all the content for the book.

Sujata Puranik Rakhra: A creative genius, she has been my sounding board and mentor through the entire creative process.

And of course, my husband, **Som**, my children **Nidhi**, **Tarang**, and **Siddharth**, who have been my pillars of strength and encouragement through this culinary journey of self-realization.

INTRODUCTION

Around the globe, the popularity of both Indian cuisine and vegetarianism is rising steadily. This book will introduce you to the joys of cooking and even show you how it can actually be a relaxing activity. Arming you with simple methods, this book will enable you to recreate the intricate flavors, intoxicating aromas, and succulent textures of homey Indian food.

I have been conducting cooking classes in Bangalore, India for over 15 years and it has been one of my most rewarding experiences. My many students have been a source of encouragement and inspiration for writing this book.

The recipes in this book have the characteristic flavor of my native province—Uttar Pradesh. My emphasis has been on crafting delicately spiced dishes, contrary to the hot flavors stereotypically associated with Indian cuisine.

Combinations of these recipes make for delicious menus and well-balanced meals. You will find numerous ways to combine courses from the many soups, salads, refreshing drinks, entrées, and scrumptious desserts featured in this book.

I have had the opportunity to perfect these recipes over the years. With these dishes, I have also tried to illustrate the immense visual appeal of Indian food and highlight the natural appeal of the freshest ingredients. The preparations for these recipes involve very simple and easy-to-understand steps. Photographs accompany all the recipes and highlight each step of the process.

I hope you and your loved ones enjoy cooking these dishes as much as I have enjoyed writing this book.

Vidhu Mittal

DISCOVER SPICES

Spices are indispensable additions used to enhance the flavor, aroma, and color of a dish. They may be used whole, or powdered in their natural form or after sun-drying. The real flavor of a spice is enhanced when it is either first toasted or dry-fried or when added before the cooking process.

 **Asafoetida** (*hing*): Obtained from the resin of a plant, this spice has a strong odor and flavor. Usually—just a pinch, added as the first ingredient to the seasoning—infuses the entire dish. It is a natural digestive aid and is easily available in powdered or lump form. Due to its strong odor it must be stored separately, away from other spices.

 Bay leaf (*tej patta*): An aromatic herb, bay leaf is also known as laurel leaf. Usually 2-3 leaves are gently heated in oil, before the addition of other ingredients, so that their subtle, fragrant aroma and flavor infuses the entire dish. It is used to season certain rice dishes and Mughlai curries. As bay leaves are inedible, they are often removed before serving.

Black cardamom (*badi elaichi*): This robust and highly aromatic spice is dark brown with tough, wrinkly skin. Used whole or crushed, it exudes a smoky, camphor-like flavor when cooked. It is used in soups, rice, curries, and lentils and is also a key ingredient of the Indian spice mix, *garam masala*. The whole pod is usually discarded while eating.

 Black peppercorn (*sabut kali mirch*): This is the sun-dried berry of the pepper plant. It can be used whole or freshly ground and adds a pleasing pungency to a variety of dishes, including soups, salads, pastas, and casseroles. It is one of the main ingredients of the Indian spice mix, *garam masala*.

 Carom seeds (*ajwain*): These are small, pale, khaki-brown seeds that are highly aromatic, with a slight pungent flavor. Usually used whole, just a little added to the seasoning is enough to flavor the entire dish. They are also used to flavor some Indian breads and pickles. Carom seeds aid in digestion.

 Cinnamon (*dalchini*): This aromatic spice is the bark of a tree, and is sold as quills, sticks, or in powdered form. It is dark, reddish-brown with a woody aroma and a warm, bittersweet flavor. Whole cinnamon is usually added to the seasoning of gravies and pilafs. It is also used to spice soups, stews, cakes, and desserts as well as some drinks, marinades, and dressings.

 Clove (*laung*): Dark brown in color, cloves are dried flower buds that are highly aromatic and have a sharp, tingly flavor. Almost always used whole and in moderation, they are added to flavor both sweet and savory dishes. Cloves are used in the preparation of the Indian spice mix, *garam masala*.

 Coriander (*dhaniya*) **seeds**: These greenish-brown seeds are the dried fruit of the cilantro (or coriander) plant. The seeds have an earthy, nutty aroma and a mild, savory flavor, very different from fresh cilantro. They are available both whole and powdered, and are used extensively in Indian cooking.

 Cumin (*jeera*) **seeds**: These are small, elongated seeds that have a distinctive warm, slightly bitter flavor when raw. Cumin seeds emit their own earthy flavor after being gently sautéed in oil. They can also be toasted and ground and dusted on yogurt dishes like *raitas*.

 Fennel (*saunf*) **seeds**: These are small, aromatic light-green seeds that have a sweet flavor. They are available both whole and powdered. Ground fennel seeds are used in savory dishes, curries, and pickles. Whole, toasted fennel seeds are often chewed as a breath freshener.

Fenugreek seeds (*methi dana*): These seeds are hard and pale yellow in color with a distinctive bitter taste. They are used both whole and powdered. When used in seasonings, only a few seeds are added, which infuse the entire dish with a warm, penetrating aroma. They are also used to flavor pickles and chutneys.

Green cardamom (*choti elaichi*): This highly fragrant spice is a light green pod containing tiny, black seeds. Usually the pod is either used whole or lightly crushed to flavor pilafs and biryanis. The seeds are often freshly ground and added to tea, rich curries, and desserts, to which they lend a sweet flavor and distinctive, refreshing aroma. Whole, they are also served as a breath freshener.

Mango powder (*amchur*): Raw, sour, green mangoes are sun dried and powdered to produce this beige-colored, fine powder with a slightly fibrous texture. It has a warm tanginess and is slightly sweet. A small quantity is usually added to vegetable dishes towards the end of the cooking process. Adding it any earlier may lengthen the cooking time.

Mint (*pudina*) **powder:** This is the sun-dried, powdered form of the fresh herb. It has a highly concentrated aroma and flavor and must be used sparingly. Just a little can lend a refreshing twist to drinks, dry vegetable dishes, Indian breads, and curries. Mint powder must be stored in a dry, airtight container and can last for up to a month.

Mustard seeds (*rai*): These are the small, round seeds of the mustard plant and come in three colors, black, brown, and yellow. The seeds are an integral part of the initial seasoning of many South Indian dishes. Mustard powder is used in certain pickles to lend a tangy, sour flavor. Mustard paste and powder are also used to add a distinct zing to dips and salad dressings.

Nutmeg (*jaiphal*): The hard, oval-shaped nutmeg seed is greyish-brown in color with a rough surface. It is aromatic and has a warm, spicy-sweet flavor and must be used sparingly. It is best used freshly grated, although powdered nutmeg is available. It is usually used to flavor vegetables, soups, and cakes.

Red chili powder (*lal mirch*): It is a hot spice prepared from ground red chilies and is added to most Indian dishes. The heat depends on the variety of red chili used. Powdered Kashmiri red chilies are comparatively less spicy and primarily used to add color, rather than heat to a dish.

Saffron (*kesar*): Saffron strands are the dried stigmas of the saffron crocus flower. They are usually infused in hot milk and gently muddled to extract their color and delicate flavor. Just a little is enough to flavor an entire dish. Highly prized, it adds a royal touch to certain rice and dessert preparations.

Sesame (*til*) **seeds:** These are tiny, flat seeds that vary in color, from creamy white to black. In India, the white variety is most commonly used. The seeds have a nutty flavor that is accentuated when toasted. The toasted seeds are used as a crunchy and flavorful garnish, and also to make certain desserts.

Turmeric (*haldi*) **powder:** Turmeric is root resembling fresh ginger. Powdered turmeric is used in most Indian dishes, to which it adds an earthy flavor and bright yellow color. Its excellent preservative properties make it an ideal addition to certain Indian pickles. Turmeric also acts as an anti-bacterial agent.

White poppyseeds (*khus khus*): Procured from the poppy plant, poppyseeds are crunchy and have a delicate, sweet aroma. They are usually ground to a smooth paste and added to curries, to which they add texture and a subtle, nutty flavor. They may also be used whole, as a light coating, before frying.

KNOW YOUR HERBS & VEGETABLES

HERBS & LEAFY GREENS

 Basil, sweet: Also known as Thai basil, the leaves of this herb are lush green and have a warm, clove-like flavor and heady aroma. Tearing basil leaves by hand is recommended over chopping. Used extensively in Asian cuisines, basil is added to flavor some drinks, soups, salads, and side dishes. In India, holy basil or *tulsi* is considered a sacred plant.

 Celery: With light green, firm stalks and dark green, ribbed leaves, celery stalks have a juicy, crunchy texture and mild herbal aftertaste. Often, the stalks are enjoyed as crudités, in health drinks, salads, and soups, while the leaves are used as a garnish. Celery is rich in vitamin A.

 Cilantro / Coriander (*hara dhaniya*): Fresh cilantro leaves range in color from light to dark green and have long stems. The tender stems and leaves are fragrant and have a refreshing flavor. Cilantro is best enjoyed fresh, in Indian condiments like chutneys or as a garnish. The herb must be stored in an airtight container in the refrigerator. A nutritional powerhouse, cilantro is a good source of vitamins, minerals, and dietary fiber.

 Curry leaves (*kadhi patta*): These are the shiny, green leaves of the curry leaf tree and are an integral spice in all south Indian cuisines. Curry leaves are usually added as part of the initial seasoning, so that their strong aroma and unique flavor infuses the entire dish. They are a rich source of vitamin C and anti-oxidants.

 Fenugreek leaves (*methi*): This fresh herb has deep green leaves and a characteristic, powerful aroma. The leaves have a pleasantly bitter flavor and can be an acquired taste. They are available dried or fresh, and they are usually used sparingly because of their concentrated flavor. Fenugreek leaves are used in curries, lentils, and certain Indian breads. This low-calorie herb is packed with vitamins and minerals.

 Lambsquarters (*bathua*): Also known as white goosefoot, pigweed, and fat hen, these leaves are dark green with uneven, jagged edges. They have warming properties and an earthy flavor that is enhanced by steaming. Lambsquarters are used to make delicacies like *Bathua Raita* (see p. 154) and *Bajra Bathua Paratha* (see p. 148). The leaves are rich in vitamins, minerals, and fiber. If you can't find them, substitute baby spinach.

 Lettuce: This popular salad green is available in a variety of colors, shapes, and flavors. In India, the most commonly used varieties are romaine and iceberg lettuce and arugula. Fresh lettuce has crisp leaves that show no signs of wilting. Immersing the leaves in cold water before use helps renew their freshness. Low in calories and packed with vitamins, lettuce is used in salads and sandwiches and even as a garnish.

 Mint (*pudina*): This aromatic herb, with intense green leaves and purple-tinged stems has a mild, peppery flavor. It is available fresh, dried, and as an extract. In India, mint is used extensively to make condiments, including chutneys and sauces, to flavor salads, soups, rice, and vegetable dishes, beverages, and ice creams. Mint sprigs are popularly used as a garnish.

Parsley: This lush green herb is available in two main varieties—curly leaf and Italian flat leaf. In India, parsley is often mistaken for cilantro. Parsley leaves have a distinctive, fresh, slightly peppery flavor, and are used to flavor soups and salads. They are also added to potato and rice dishes. Parsley is rich in vitamins A and C.

 **Spinach** (*palak*): These crisp, dark green leaves have a robust, earthy flavor and a slightly bitter aftertaste. Young spinach leaves are often enjoyed raw in salads. Spinach may be steamed or sautéed and then added to vegetable or lentil dishes. They may also be added to soups, casseroles, and rice dishes. Spinach leaves are a rich source of iron as well as vitamins A and C.

 **Scallions** (*hara pyaz*): Also known as spring or salad onions, this variety of onion has edible, long, firm, green stalks and small, white bulbs. The outer layer of the bulb is usually peeled before using. They are milder flavored than regular onions and are added to salads, soups, stir-fries, rice, and vegetable dishes. They are also used as a garnish.

GREEN VEGETABLES

 **Asparagus** (*shatwar*): This delicate, seasonal vegetable resembles little spears and is available in green, white, and purple varieties. Asparagus spears may have tough stems that need to be peeled. Their subtle flavor is often enjoyed by simply sautéing in butter or olive oil. They are also used in soups, salads, pizzas, and rice dishes. Asparagus is rich in vitamin A.

 Bell pepper (*Shimla mirch*): This bell-shaped vegetable comes in a variety of sizes and colors, most commonly, green, red, and yellow. They are firm with glossy skin and have a watery crunch. Green bell peppers have a fresh, mildly piquant flavor, whereas the red, yellow, and orange varieties tend to be sweeter. Bell peppers may be enjoyed both raw or cooked, and can be used in soups, salads, stir-fries, casseroles, and side dishes. They are a rich source of vitamin C.

 Bottle gourd (*lauki*): Also known as calabash, this vegetable has light green, shiny skin with white flesh and edible seeds. It has a subtle flavor and is used to make soups, side dishes, and even desserts. Bottle gourd is a rich source of dietary fiber, and is consumed as a juice for its therapeutic properties.

 Broccoli: This vegetable has deep, emerald green flower heads, attached to stout stems. Broccoli can be blanched, steamed, sautéed, or fried and is used in soups, salads, casseroles, and side dishes. It can also be enjoyed blanched or raw as a healthy snack, accompanied by a dip. Broccoli is a good source of vitamins A and C, as well as riboflavin, calcium, and iron.

 Cucumber (*khira*): This is a long, cylindrical vegetable that varies in size from small to large and in color from light to dark green. It has smooth skin and crisp, juicy flesh. Cucumber has a refreshing flavor, but sometimes can leave a slightly bitter aftertaste. It can be served in crudités and drinks, added to salads, sandwiches, cold soups, and *raitas*. Baby cucumbers are often pickled. Cucumbers aid digestion and are a good source of vitamins A and C, and minerals.

Green bananas / Plantains (*kacha kela*): Also known as raw bananas, these have a smooth, bright green skin that sheathes firm and starchy flesh. The flesh is not sweet (unless very ripe), but does have a subtle banana flavor. It cannot be eaten uncooked. Green bananas are used to make fries, kebabs, soups, stews, and other vegetable dishes. They are highly nutritious and rich in dietary fiber and vitamins A and C.

Green chili (*hari mirch*): This fiery little vegetable has green, shiny, smooth skin and is available in many varieties that differ in shape, size, and pungency. Green chilies can be made into a paste, chopped, slit, or added whole. To tone down their pungency, deseed the chilies before use. Plump, green chilies are often used to make chili pickle. They are rich in vitamin C.

Green peas (*hara mattar*): Fresh peas come nestled within bright, glossy green pods and are mildly sweet. They can be paired with a number of vegetables and added to salads, soups, rice dishes, and stuffings. Available both fresh and frozen, they have a fair amount of vitamins A and C, and iron.

Green beans: These beans are deep green and slender with smooth skin. They are tender and crisp with a hint of sweetness. They can be used in soups, salads, rice dishes, and other vegetable dishes. These beans are also known as *haricot vert*, which is the French name for green string beans.

Okra (*bhindi*): Also known as ladies finger, this vegetable is a firm, dark green pod with ridged skin. When cut, it reveals edible, white seeds and a sticky texture. Okra must be washed and dried thoroughly before cooking, as moisture causes the pods to become slimy. A popular vegetable in Indian cuisine, it is used to make fritters, and also in side dishes and *raitas*. This low-calorie vegetable is a rich source of dietary fiber, vitamins, and minerals.

Zucchini: This cylindrical vegetable is available in green and yellow varieties. Both have shiny, edible outer skin and white flesh that has a delicate flavor. Zucchini can be steamed, grilled, sautéed, or deep-fried. However, as it cooks quickly, monitoring the cooking time is essential. It is popularly used in soups, salads, casseroles, and rice dishes.

ROOT VEGETABLES

Carrot (*gajar*): This root vegetable has feathery, bitter-tasting leaves and a long, slender root that can range in color from orange and red to purple. Tender carrots are crisp with a sweet flavor. Carrots can be used to make drinks, soups, salads, side dishes, rice dishes, and desserts. They are a rich source of carotene and vitamin A.

Ginger (*adrak*): This knobbly root is pale beige with smooth skin and fibrous flesh. It has a warm, peppery flavor and robust aroma. Integral to Indian cooking, ginger is added to both sweet and savory dishes and is also used to spice cookies, cakes, and tea. Tender ginger is often pickled. Ginger aids digestion and has warming properties.

Potato (*aloo*): This starchy, tuberous root vegetable comes in a variety of shapes, sizes, and colors. In India, the most commonly used potato varieties vary in color from light beige to dark brown. Used extensively in Indian cooking, the delicious and versatile potato can be boiled, baked, or deep-fried and is used in soups, salads, appetizers, snacks, and main courses.

Radish (*mooli*): There are two main varieties of this root vegetable. One is white and long with small, smooth roots protruding from its skin, and the other is an oval, red-skinned variety. Raw radish is crisp and juicy with a flavor that can range from mildly pungent to sharp. Radish is used in salads, pickles, and side dishes and to stuff Indian breads. It is a good source of dietary fiber, vitamins, and minerals.

Turnip (*shalgam*): This plump root vegetable has white skin, often with a purple-tinged top and creamy white flesh. Baby turnips have a subtle, sweet flavor and are best enjoyed raw in salads or as crudités. The mature vegetable tends to have a sharp flavor and is usually used in pickles and side dishes. Turnips are a good source of vitamin C.

MISCELLANEOUS

 Eggplant / Aubergine (*baingan*): This vegetable comes in various shapes and sizes and varies in color from white and green to dark purple. They have edible skin and seeds, and sponge-like flesh. Usually tender eggplants are preferred over the mature ones, as the latter tends to have dark, bitter seeds. They can be baked, grilled, or fried and also used to make dips, stews, side dishes, and rice dishes.

 **Baby corn** (*chotte bhutte*): This is harvested, premature corn that looks like miniature corn on the cob. Fresh baby corn is tender with a crisp texture and has a subtle, mildly sweet flavor. It is usually consumed whole. Baby corn is used in soups, salads, stir-fries, fritters, casseroles, and side dishes. It is available both fresh and canned. Baby corn is a good source of vitamins C and B6 as well as folate, potassium, and fiber.

 Baby onion: Also known as pearl or button onions. These pearl-shaped bulbs have an inedible, thin, paper-like skin and can range in color from white to pink. They have a sweet, delicate flavor and delicious crunch. Usually used whole, they are added to rice and lentil dishes, soups, salads, and casseroles. Pickled baby onions are a popular condiment.

 Cabbage (*bandh gobi*): This is a vegetable with a globular head of waxy, crisp leaves, which are curly or flat. The leaves can range in color from almost white to green. Cabbage can be used in salads, soups, side dishes, and even to stuff Indian breads. It is a good source of vitamin C.

 Cauliflower (*phool gobi*): This vegetable has green leaves enveloping tightly-packed white florets that are attached to stout stalks. Raw cauliflower is crunchy and sweet. It can be used to make soups, fritters, casseroles, side dishes, rice dishes, and to stuff Indian breads. Cauliflower is low in fat and high in dietary fiber and vitamin C.

 Cherry tomato: This is the smaller version of the tomato and is usually round or oblong with shiny, smooth skin that can vary in color from red to orange to yellow. Sweeter than its larger cousin, cherry tomatoes are either used whole or halved, and are best enjoyed raw in salads. They are often used as a garnish and even added to certain side dishes.

 Garlic (*lasan*): Each garlic bulb is made up of many individual pearly white cloves. Raw garlic has a strong odor and flavor that is further released when it is chopped or crushed. Usually paired with ginger in Indian cuisine, when cooked, garlic becomes sweeter and less pungent, infusing its flavor into the entire dish. It is also added to salad dressings and used to make pickles. Packed with medicinal benefits, garlic is considered a natural wonder drug.

 Jackfruit (*kathal*): This large, oval-shaped tropical fruit has an inedible, thick, prickly skin. The flesh and seeds of tender, unripened jackfruit make for nutritious curries and rice dishes. Pickled, it is a delicacy in northern India. The ripe fruit has sweet, golden flesh with a strong aroma and is an acquired taste.

 Indian water chestnut (*singhada*): This seasonal fruit has a firm, greenish-brown, outer cover and white flesh, which has a subtle, sweet flavor and crunchy texture. Water chestnuts can be enjoyed raw. They can also be sautéed, grilled, or baked and added to soups, salads, side dishes, and rice dishes. They are available fresh in season, as well as canned, and are a good source of vitamin C and minerals.

 **Lemon** (*nimbu*): Lemons are round or oblong citrus fruits with firm glossy rinds. They range in color from greenish to bright yellow. Their tangy juice is used to flavor certain teas, drinks, soups, and side dishes, while their rind is often added to flavor cakes and desserts. Lemon slices and wedges are popularly used to garnish drinks. In India, lemons are also used to prepare pickles. They are a rich source of vitamin C.

 **Lotus stem** (*kamal kakdi*): Also known as lotus root, this vegetable has reddish-brown skin that must be peeled before using. Its flesh is creamy-white and crisp. Lotus stems are used to make kebabs, side dishes, and pickles. They can also be added to salads or made into fritters. Pick lotus stems that are white with closed ends, as the open-ended ones tend to be muddy inside. They are a rich source of dietary fiber, vitamins, and minerals.

 Mushroom (*khumb*): Mushrooms are fleshy fungi that come in a variety of shapes and sizes. The most commonly used in Indian cooking is the cultivated white mushroom. When fresh, they have white caps with few blemishes. They can be used in dips and sauces, soups, salads, toppings, curries, and for fritters. Use fresh mushrooms within 1-2 days, as they tend to have a short shelf life and blacken quickly.

 Olive (*jaitoon*): This small fruit contains a pit and comes in a variety of colors and sizes, each with its own distinct flavor. Green olives are the young fruit, while black olives are the mature, tree-ripened fruit. Olives need to be cured before being eaten. They are often served with cheese (as an appetizer), used in pizza toppings, salads, and also as a garnish. They are also used to obtain olive oil. Full of health benefits, olives are a good source of vitamin E and anti-oxidants.

 Onion (*pyaz*): This fleshy, round vegetable has a paper-like covering and comes in many varieties, including red, white, and yellow. Raw onions have a very sharp odor and pungency. However, when cooked, they lend a delicate aroma and depth to the dish. Integral to most Indian gravies, they are also added to lentils, rice dishes, stuffing, soups, salads, and garnishes. They are a good source of vitamin C.

 Sweet corn kernels (*makai*): These golden yellow kernels are soft and sweet and can be eaten directly off the cob, after steaming or grilling. They can also be enjoyed as a topping or stuffing, in soups, salads, curries, and in fritters. Available fresh, canned, or frozen, they are a good source of vitamins and carbohydrates.

 Tomato (*tamatar*): Tomatoes are juicy and plump with smooth, shiny skins that range in color from red and green to yellow. They come in many different shapes and sizes with flavors varying from sweet to tart. Tomatoes are an integral ingredient in Indian sauce bases and are also used as a garnish and topping, as well as to make juices, soups, sauces, salads, and sandwiches. Tomatoes are a good source of Vitamins A and C.

FRUITS

Grape (*angoor*): This is a plump, juicy fruit that grows in bunches on vines, and comes in a variety of sizes, colors, and flavors. Grapes are mainly used to make wine. Their crispy texture and sweet, slightly tart flavor also makes them a great addition to custards, ice cream, and salads. They are also used to make jams and jellies. Grapes are rich in dietary fiber, vitamin A, and minerals.

Kiwi: This is an oblong fruit with downy, brownish-green skin. It has vibrant, deep green flesh with small, crunchy, edible black seeds. Kiwi fruit is enjoyed for its distinctive sweet-tart flavor. It is often added to salads, puréed into a refreshing drink, and used as a garnish. Kiwi fruit is an excellent source of vitamin C.

Pear (*nashpati*): There are many types of pears and they come in a variety of shapes (from bell-shaped to spherical), colors (from green and red to golden yellow), and textures (soft or crisp). Their flavor can range from sweet to tart-sweet. Pears can be stewed, used in salads and desserts, or even added to drinks.

Pineapple (*ananas*): This is a juicy, tropical fruit with a raised, diamond pattern on its golden-brown skin. Its sweet, tangy flavor is enjoyed in salads, certain gravies, desserts, and cakes. It can also be used to make juice, preserves, and jams. Pineapple is available fresh, canned, or dried.

Pomegranate (*anar*): This is a round fruit with leathery, red-gold skin. Its edible seeds are sheathed in juicy, translucent flesh and have a flavor ranging from sweet to tart, and a color ranging from white and pale pink to ruby red. They can be used as a garnish, added to salads and *raitas*, and can also be crushed and made into juice. They are a rich source of potassium and anti-oxidants. Dried and powdered pomegranate seed is a popular Indian flavoring.

Strawberry: This conical-shaped fruit belongs to the rose family and comes in various sizes. Its color ranges from pale orange to bright red and its flavor from sweet to tart. Strawberries can be eaten raw or made into desserts, preserves, and sauces. Fresh strawberries have a short-shelf life and are best when ripe. Strawberries are an excellent source of vitamin C.

NUTS

Almonds (*badam*): This nut may be used whole, ground, or slivered and is popularly sprinkled as a garnish on Indian desserts. Often, skinned almonds are crushed into a paste and used to thicken curries, to which they lend a rich, creamy texture and mild, sweet flavor. Almonds are a rich source of protein and vitamin E.

Almondettes (*chironji*): These tiny seeds come from the *Buchanania lanzan* tree. They are pale brown and round, with a flat surface on one side, and come encased in a hard shell. Almondettes are usually added to desserts. As the seeds have a high oil content, they must be kept refrigerated and used before they turn rancid.

Cashew nuts (*kaju*): A creamy white, kidney-shaped nut, cashews have a mild, buttery flavor and crumbly texture. Cashew nut paste is often used to thicken and flavor certain rich Indian gravies. Lightly fried or toasted cashew nuts are enjoyed as a savory snack, and are often added to rice dishes and desserts.

Dates (*khajoor*): A dried fruit that comes from the date palm tree, dates have a honey-sweetness and are enjoyed both ripe and semi-dried. They make a delicious addition to cakes, dips, and chutneys. Plump dates stuffed with nuts are a specialty dessert. Dates are a good source of dietary fiber.

Fox nuts (*makhana*): Also known as gorgon nuts, fox nuts are the seeds of a flowering plant that belongs to the water lily family. Fox nuts are white with a few dark spots. They are used to make sweet and savory Indian delicacies, including a delicious toasted snack, seasoned with salt and pepper. Fox nuts have medicinal and anti-oxidant properties.

Pine nuts / Pignolias (*chilgoza*): Ivory-colored and slender, pine nuts have a thin, soft, brown shell and are often toasted to accentuate their natural, nutty flavor. The unique crunch and flavor of pine nuts are used to enhance many rice, vegetable, and dessert dishes. They must be used fresh, as the older nuts tend to turn bitter. Pine nuts are packed with protein and fiber and are a rich source of anti-oxidants, vitamins A and E, and niacin.

Pistachios (*pista*): Pale green and encased in a hard, beige shell, pistachios can be used—whole, ground, chopped, or slivered—as a garnish or dessert flavoring. They are packed with vitamins, minerals, and anti-oxidants and are also a good source of protein. Salted pistachios make for a delicious snack.

Raisins (*kishmish*): Raisins are dried grapes and are available in a number of varieties. They range in color from golden and dark plum to black. They are used in certain Indian desserts and condiments as well as cakes and cookies. Raisins are a rich source of iron, vitamins, and anti-oxidants.

Walnuts (*akhrot*): Walnuts are available shelled, chopped, or whole. Shelled nuts are soft with an appealing, bittersweet flavor. Commonly eaten as a snack, they are also added to salads, cakes, and cookies. Walnuts are a good source of protein and dietary fiber. If kept in a cool, dry place, they can be stored for up to 3 months.

THE GOODNESS OF LENTILS

In India, lentils are usually soaked and pressure-cooked. Their cooking time depends on the variety of lentil. They are used in salads, soups, curries, and vegetable or rice dishes. Desserts are also made from certain lentil varieties. Lentils are packed with protein, fiber, and they are low in calories. They also contain folic acid, potassium, iron, and magnesium. Store lentils in airtight containers.

Highly nutritious, pulses or lentils are an intrinsic part of most Indian cuisines, with at least one lentil dish featuring in the daily menu of most homes. Lentils or *dal* come in many varieties; they range in shape, size, and color, with as many variations in flavor and texture. Lentils are usually available whole, split, and with or without skin.

Split green lentil
(Dhuli moong dal)

Red gram lentils
(Malka masoor dal)

Split green gram lentils
(Chilka moong dal)

Husked split Bengal gram
(Chana dal)

Whole green gram lentils
(Sabut moong dal)

Black gram
(Kala chana)

Husked split black lentil
(Dhuli urad dal)

Kidney beans
(Rajmah)

Whole black gram
(Sabut urad dal)

DRINKS, SOUPS, & SALADS

TENDER COCO-BERRY REFRESHER
Strawberry Malaika

Makes 1 glass (225 ml)

 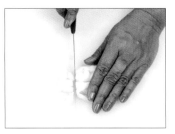  

THE EXOTIC BLEND OF TROPICAL AND TEMPERATE FRUIT GIVES THIS DRINK ITS DELICIOUS TEXTURE, FLAVOR, AND PRETTY CHERRY-BLOSSOM COLOR.

INGREDIENTS

1 cup / 200 ml Tender coconut water (*daab*)
½ cup / 50 g Strawberries, chopped
2 tbsp / 30 g Tender coconut cream (*daab ki malai*), chopped
¼ tsp Chopped parsley
1 tbsp / 15 ml Sugar syrup (see p. 217)

To garnish:
A few Strawberry slices
1 Parsley sprig

METHOD

- Chill the tender coconut water, strawberries, and coconut cream.

- Blend the tender coconut water, strawberries, coconut cream, parsley, and sugar syrup to a coarse purée in a blender / food processor.

- Pour into a serving glass and garnish with strawberry slices and a sprig of parsley; serve immediately.

- Tender coconut water is a cooling, therapeutic beverage that is considered the perfect, natural thirst quencher.

- The thin, pulpy flesh (cream) of the coconut is usually eaten after drinking the water.

ROSE YOGURT SHAKE
Lassi Gulbahar

INGREDIENTS
½ cup / 100 g Thick plain yogurt (*dahi*)
¼ cup / 50 ml Chilled milk
2½ tbsp / 40 g Confectioner's or powdered sugar (see p. 217)
1 tsp / 5 ml Rose water (*gulab jal*)
4 Red rose petals, about 1" in size
8-10 Ice cubes

To garnish:
A few Rose petals, whole or shredded
½ tsp Almonds (*badam*), peeled, slivered (see p. 218)
½ tsp Pistachios (*pista*), peeled, slivered (see p. 218)

METHOD
- Blend the yogurt, chilled milk, sugar, rose water, and rose petals with the ice cubes to a smooth consistency in a blender or food processor.

- Pour into a glass.

- Serve chilled, garnished with rose petals and slivered almonds and pistachios.

THE TEXTURE OF THE PETALS, BLENDED WITH THE YOGURT, ENHANCES THE UNIQUE FLAVOR OF THIS DAYTIME SUMMER COOLER.

- Yogurt that has been kept in the refrigerator for one day is ideal for this recipe. Avoid using the whey, as it alters both the flavor and texture of this drink.

- Rose water is a distillate from rose petals, and is used in certain Indian recipes for its unique aroma and flavor.

PINEAPPLE KIWI COOLER
Ananas Kiwi Sharbat

INGREDIENTS
3 oz / 75 g Pineapple (*ananas*),
cut into 1" pieces (¾ cup)
1 tsp / 5 g Chopped ginger
(*adrak*)
2½ tbsp / 40 g Sugar
1 oz / 25 g Kiwi fruit, chopped
(¼ cup)
4 Mint (*pudina*) leaves
4 Ice cubes
Chilled club soda, to top up
To garnish:
2 thin Pineapple pieces
2 thin Kiwi fruit slices

METHOD
• Place the pineapple pieces,
ginger, sugar, and ¼ cup /
50 ml water in a pan and
bring to a boil on low heat;
simmer for 5 minutes, stirring
occasionally. Turn off the heat
and set aside to cool.

• Blend the cooled mixture to
a smooth consistency in a
blender / food processor;
strain and refrigerate the
pineapple juice.

• **To serve**, coarsely crush the chopped kiwi pieces with the mint
leaves in a mortar and pestle.

• Place the ice cubes in a glass and add the crushed kiwi and mint
mixture. Add the chilled pineapple juice and top with club soda.

• Skewer the pineapple pieces and kiwi slices on a long toothpick
and place resting on the rim of the glass. Serve immediately.

THE
ADDITION OF KIWI,
WITH A HINT OF MINT,
ADDS A ZING TO THIS
SWEET-TART PINEAPPLE
COOLER.

• Pineapple juice can be made in advance. Refrigerate and use
within six hours.

PIQUANT PEAR
Raseeli Nashpati

Makes 1 glass (125 ml)

METHOD

- Peel and core the pear and cut into cubes. Mix the pear cubes, sugar, and 1 cup / 200 ml water in a pan; add the cinnamon stick and the lemon pieces.

- Bring the mixture to a boil on low heat and cook until the sugar dissolves, stirring occasionally. Turn off the heat and set aside to cool. Remove the cinnamon stick and reserve for use later.

- Blend the cooled pear mixture to a smooth consistency in a blender / food processor; strain, discard the pulp, and refrigerate the juice.

- **To serve,** fill half the glass with ice cubes and add the julienned lemon zest. Pour in the chilled juice and add the reserved cinnamon stick. Garnish with the mint sprig and lemon slice; serve immediately.

THE DELICATE, SWEET SPICED FLAVOR OF CINNAMON IS PERFECT FOR THIS FRUITY REFRESHMENT.

INGREDIENTS

1 / 175 g Yellow Bartlett pear
2½ tbsp / 40 g Sugar
1" Cinnamon (*dalchini*) stick
3 Lemon (*nimbu*) wedges, ¼" in size, deseeded
To garnish:
Ice cubes
4-5 Strips of julienne lemon zest (see tip)
1 Mint (*pudina*) sprig
1 Lemon slice

- Fruits like bananas, apples, and pears discolor after they are peeled. To avoid darkening, prepare the pear cubes just before use.

- To obtain julienne lemon zest, peel the rind of a fresh lemon with a sharp knife and cut into thin strips.

POMEGRANATE PUNCH
Anari Punch

INGREDIENTS

4 tbsp / 60 ml Pomegranate juice (*anar ka ras*), fresh, extracted from 1 cup / 150 g pomegranate seeds
1 tbsp / 15 ml Sugar syrup (see p. 217)
1 tsp / 5 ml White vinegar (*safed sirka*)
½ tsp / 2½ ml Bitters (Angostura)
1 cup Crushed ice
Chilled club soda, to top up

To garnish:

1 Apple (*seb*) slice
1 Cucumber (*khira*) slice
2-4 Basil leaves

METHOD

• Using a juicer, extract the juice from the pomegranate seeds and strain through a sieve.

• Place the pomegranate juice in a serving glass and add the sugar syrup, white vinegar, and bitters; stir gently.

• Add the crushed ice and top with chilled club soda; stir gently again. Add the apple and cucumber slices and drop in the basil leaves. Serve chilled.

THE SECRET HERB AND SPICE FORMULA OF THE BITTERS, ALONG WITH THE WHITE VINEGAR, BRINGS OUT THE SWEET-TARTNESS OF POMEGRANATE JUICE IN THIS VIBRANT MOCKTAIL.

• To achieve the perfect color and flavor of this drink, choose the pomegranate variety with dark red seeds.

• Bitters is a liquid made by distilling a mixture of plants, roots, aromatic herbs, and even barks. It lends a unique, bitter-sweet flavor to any mocktail.

GREEN BREEZER
Angoori Hara Panna

INGREDIENTS

3 oz / 75 g Green grapes (*angoor*), seedless, chopped (½ cup)

1 oz / 25 g Cucumber (*khira*), chopped (¼ cup)

¼ cup (tightly-packed) Iceberg lettuce, torn by hand

½ tsp Chopped celery stalks, (see p. 211)

⅛ tsp Mustard (*sarson*) powder

½ tsp / 2½ g Chopped ginger (*adrak*)

2 Lemon (*nimbu*) wedges, ½" in size, deseeded

1¼ tbsp / 20 ml Sugar syrup (see p. 217)

¾ cup / 150 ml Chilled water

4-6 Ice cubes

To garnish:

2-3 Celery leaves

A few Seedless green grapes, sliced

METHOD

• Blend the green grapes, cucumber, lettuce leaves, celery stalks, mustard powder, ginger, lemon pieces, sugar syrup, and water to a smooth consistency in a blender / food processor.

• Strain the mixture through a sieve and discard the pulp.

• Place the ice cubes, celery leaves, and a few chopped grapes in a glass and pour in the drink mixture; serve immediately.

THE REFRESHING TANG OF THIS DRINK IS ACCENTUATED BY THE SUBTLE FLAVORS OF GINGER AND MUSTARD.

• Discard a few of the outer leaves of the lettuce before using.
• To prepare mustard powder, dry-grind yellow / white mustard seeds to a fine powder in a spice grinder.

POTATO CAULIFLOWER POTTAGE
Phool Gobi Aloo Shorba

INGREDIENTS
1 cup / 100 g Cauliflower (*phool gobi*) florets
1 medium / 75 g Potato, chopped
1 tsp / 5 g Butter
1 tsp / 5 g Ginger (*adrak*) paste (see p. 206)
2 tsp / 10 g Cilantro (*dhaniya*) paste (see p. 207)
Salt to taste
Black peppercorns (*sabut kali mirch*), freshly ground, to taste

To garnish:
2 tsp / 10 g Butter
2 tbsp / 30 g Paneer, grated (see p. 204)

METHOD
- Pressure-cook the cauliflower florets and potato with 2 cups / 475 ml water to one whistle; turn off the heat (or cook in a soup pot until tender). Once the pressure drops, open the lid and cool. Purée the mixture in a blender / food processor; strain and set aside the soup stock.

- Heat 1 tsp butter in a pan for 30 seconds; add the ginger and cilantro pastes and cook on moderate heat for 10 seconds. Add the strained soup stock and season with salt to taste; mix. Bring the soup to a boil and simmer for 2 minutes.

- **To garnish,** heat 2 tsp butter in a pan for 30 seconds; add the grated paneer, and fry on moderate heat until crisp and light brown.

- Remove and drain on absorbent paper towel.

- Transfer the soup to a serving bowl; sprinkle with freshly ground black pepper to taste and garnish with fried paneer; serve immediately.

THE CREAMY BLEND OF CAULIFLOWER AND POTATO IS COMPLEMENTED PERFECTLY BY THE CRISPY, PANEER GARNISH.

- While serving, you can add 2-3 drops of lemon juice to the soup for a delicious, tangy twist.

• Always season soups with freshly ground black pepper, as this adds immensely to the flavor and aroma of the soup.

LEAFY MUSHROOM LENTIL SOUP
Lazeez Khumb Dal Shorba

Serves: 2

INGREDIENTS

2 cups / 200 g Tender bottle gourd (*lauki*), peeled, diced
2 tbsp / 25 g Red gram lentils (*malka masoor dal*)
1 tsp / 5 g Butter
1 tsp / 5 g Finely-chopped garlic (*lasan*)
2 tbsp Finely-chopped spinach (*palak*)
2 tbsp Thinly-sliced mushrooms (*khumb*)
Salt to taste
Black peppercorns (*sabut kali mirch*), freshly ground, to taste

To garnish:

1 tsp / 5 g Butter
4 tbsp Finely-chopped spinach, washed, dried on a dish towel
1 tsp / 5 g White sesame seeds (*safed til*)

METHOD

• Wash the diced bottle gourd and red gram separately. Pressure cook the bottle gourd and red gram with 2 cups / 475 ml water to one whistle; simmer for 2 minutes and turn off the heat (or cook in a conventional pot until tender). Once the pressure drops, open the lid and cool. Blend the mixture in a blender / food processor; strain and set aside the soup stock.

• Heat 1 tsp butter in a pan for 30 seconds; add the garlic and sauté on moderate heat until light brown. Add the spinach and cook on moderate heat for 10 seconds. Add the mushrooms and sauté for 10 seconds. Add the soup stock and season with salt and freshly ground black pepper to taste. Bring the soup to a boil and simmer for 2 minutes.

• **To garnish,** heat 1 tsp butter in a pan for 30 seconds; add the spinach and sauté on moderate heat until crisp, stirring continuously. Add the white sesame seeds and cook on moderate heat for 10 seconds.

• Transfer the soup to a serving bowl, top with the spinach-sesame seed garnish, and serve immediately.

THE MODEST BOTTLE GOURD COMBINES WITH MUSHROOM, SPINACH, AND SESAME SEEDS TO CREATE AN EXCITING SOUP WITH A DELICATE, NUTTY FLAVOR.

• Use tender bottle gourd, which has a slightly downy surface and soft skin.

• You can make the soup in advance; however, prepare and add the garnish just before serving.

GREEN MEDLEY
Hariyali Shorba

Serves: 3-4

PACKED WITH A MEDLEY OF VEGETABLES, THE FLAVOR OF THIS NUTRITIOUS SOUP IS ENHANCED BY THE SUBTLE SWEETNESS OF NUTMEG.

INGREDIENTS

For the soup stock:
½ tsp / 2½ g Butter
1 oz / 25 g Baby corn (*chotte bhutte*), cut into discs (¼ cup)
2 oz / 50 g Broccoli florets, chopped (½ cup)
¼ cup / 25 g Chopped cabbage (*bandh gobi*)
¼ Bell pepper (*Shimla mirch*), cut into 1" pieces
2 medium / 150 g Potatoes, chopped

For the soup:
1 tsp / 5 g Butter
8 Basil leaves
1 oz / 25 g Baby corn, cut into discs (¼ cup)
2 oz / 50 g Broccoli florets, chopped (½ cup)
Salt to taste
Black peppercorns (*sabut kali mirch*), freshly ground, to taste
A pinch Sugar
A pinch Nutmeg (*jaiphal*), grated

METHOD

- **For the stock,** heat ½ tsp butter in a pressure cooker for 30 seconds; add the baby corn, broccoli, cabbage, pepper, and potatoes; sauté on moderate heat for 30 seconds. Add 2½ cups / 600 ml water and pressure cook to one whistle; turn off the heat (or cook in a conventional pot until tender). Once the pressure drops, open the lid and cool. Blend the mixture in a blender / food processor; strain and set aside the soup stock.

- **For the soup,** heat 1 tsp butter in a pan for 30 seconds; add the basil leaves, baby corn, and broccoli; sauté on moderate heat for 30 seconds. Add the strained soup stock, salt and freshly ground black pepper to taste, and sugar.

- Add the grated nutmeg and mix. Bring the soup mixture to a boil and simmer for 2 minutes. Serve hot.

- The soup stock can be made in advance; however, follow the final steps to prepare the soup just before serving.

- While sautéing the baby corn and broccoli for the soup, do not overcook the vegetables, as they will lose their crunch.

ZUCCHINI ASPARAGUS FIESTA
Shatawar Sabz Shorba

INGREDIENTS

¼ lb / 125 g Tender asparagus (*shatawar*) spears

2½ tsp / 12½ g Butter (1 tsp + 1 tsp + ½ tsp)

1 medium / 75 g Onion, cut into long slices

5 oz / 140 g Zucchini, sliced into ¼" semicircles (¾ cup + ¼ cup)

2 tbsp Chopped scallions (*hare pyaz ke patte*)

¼ tsp Finely-chopped garlic (*lasan*)

Salt to taste

Black peppercorns (*sabut kali mirch*), freshly ground, to taste

A pinch Sugar

METHOD

- **To prepare the asparagus (see p. 211),** cut 1" off the asparagus heads and set aside for the garnish. Shave the remaining spears with a sharp knife or asparagus peeler. Cut the tender portion of the asparagus spears into ¼" discs and set aside for the soup. Use the remaining hard ends for the soup stock.

- **For the stock,** heat 1 tsp butter in a pressure cooker for 30 seconds; add the onion slices and sauté on moderate heat for 30 seconds. Add the hard ends of the asparagus, ¾ cup zucchini slices, and scallions; mix and sauté for 30 seconds. Add 2 cups / 475 ml water and pressure cook to one whistle; turn off the heat and allow the pressure to drop. (Alternatively, follow the same method in a conventional pot, increasing the cooking times.)

- Open the lid and cool. Blend the mixture in a blender / food processor; strain and set aside the soup stock.

- **For the soup,** heat 1 tsp butter in a pan for 30 seconds; add the garlic and sauté on moderate heat for 10 seconds. Add the soft asparagus discs and the remaining ¼ cup zucchini slices; sauté for 30 seconds. Add the soup stock; season with salt and freshly ground black pepper and a pinch of sugar; mix gently. Bring the soup to a boil and simmer for 1 minute.

- **To garnish,** heat ½ tsp butter in a pan for 10 seconds. Add the asparagus heads and sauté on moderate heat for 30 seconds.

- Transfer the soup to a serving bowl, garnish with sautéed asparagus heads, and serve immediately.

- Use only fresh asparagus (green or white) that is tender, with firm stalks.

- Green zucchini, rather than yellow summer squash, is ideal for this soup.

THIS
SOUP IS A DELICIOUS
ODE TO THE KING OF VEGETABLES,
ASPARAGUS, ENHANCED BY THE
WONDERFUL AROMA OF
SCALLIONS AND
DELICATE FLAVOR OF
ZUCCHINI.

SOUP 'O' MUSHROOM
Khumbi Shorba

INGREDIENTS
4 medium / 60 g Mushrooms (*khumb*)
2 tsp / 10 g Butter (1½ tsp + ½ tsp)
¾ tsp / 4 g All-purpose flour (*maida*)
¾ cup / 150 ml Milk
1 tsp Chopped parsley
1 tsp Chopped celery stalk (see p. 211)
⅛ tsp Freshly-ground black peppercorns (*sabut kali mirch*)
¼ tsp Sugar
Salt to taste

To garnish:
¼ tsp Butter
1 medium / 15 g Mushroom, sliced
1 tsp Parsley, chopped

> THE COMBINATION OF MUSHROOMS AND CELERY GIVES THIS LIGHT SOUP DELICIOUS BODY AND CRUNCH.

METHOD
- Chop 2 mushrooms and grate the remaining 2.

- Heat 1½ tsp butter in a pan for 30 seconds; add the chopped mushrooms and all-purpose flour and sauté on moderate heat for 20 seconds; turn off the heat.

- Add the milk and ¾ cup / 150 ml water and mix. Blend the soup mixture in a blender / food processor; set aside.

- Heat ½ tsp butter in a pan for 30 seconds; add the grated mushrooms and the parsley and sauté on moderate heat for 10 seconds. Pour in the soup mixture and add the celery, black pepper, sugar, and salt to taste; mix. Bring the soup to a boil and simmer for 2 minutes. Transfer to a serving bowl.

- **To garnish,** heat ¼ tsp butter in a pan for 10 seconds; add the mushroom slices and sauté on moderate heat for 30 seconds; remove. Garnish the soup with sautéed mushrooms and parsley; serve immediately.

- Always use fresh mushrooms that are firm and white, which show no signs of discoloration.

- While the soup can be made in advance, ensure you prepare and add the garnish just before serving.

LEAFY PANEER SOUP
Pattidar Paneer Shorba

Serves: 2

THIS LIGHT
AND FLAVORFUL SOUP
CELEBRATES IN THE MYRIAD
TEXTURES OF ITS INGREDIENTS,
WHILE OFFERING THE BALANCED
GOODNESS OF PROTEIN AND
CARBOHYDRATES.

INGREDIENTS

For the soup stock:
2 oz / 50 g Cabbage (*bandh gobi*), cut into 1" cubes (½ cup)
1 medium / 75 g Potato, cut into ½" cubes

For the soup:
2 tsp / 10 ml Refined vegetable oil (1 tsp + 1 tsp)
1 oz / 30 g Paneer, cut into 8 cubes, 1" in size (see p. 204)
¼ tsp Finely-chopped ginger (*adrak*)
1 tbsp Canned or steamed corn (*makai*) kernels
Salt to taste
Black peppercorns (*sabut kali mirch*), freshly ground, to taste
A pinch Sugar
4 Spinach (*palak*) leaves

METHOD

- **For the soup stock**, pressure-cook the cabbage and potato cubes with 2½ cups / 600 ml water to one whistle; turn off the heat and allow the pressure to drop (or cook in a conventional pot until tender). Open the lid and cool. Blend the mixture in a blender / food processor; strain and set aside the soup stock.

- **For the soup,** heat 1 tsp oil in a pan for 30 seconds; add the paneer cubes and sauté on moderate heat until evenly light brown; remove and set aside.

- In a separate pan, heat 1 tsp oil; add the ginger and corn; cook on moderate heat for 10 seconds. Add the sautéed paneer cubes, soup stock, salt and freshly ground pepper to taste, and sugar; mix gently. Bring the soup to a boil, add the spinach leaves, and cook on moderate heat for 10 seconds. Serve immediately.

- To save time, you may use packaged paneer, which is easily available in Indian supermarkets.

PEAR 'N' NUT SALAD
Nashpati Singhara Salaad

THE SUBTLE FLAVORS OF GINGER AND MINT PERFECTLY COMPLEMENT THE JUICY CRUNCH OF THE WATER CHESTNUTS AND THE SWEET CRISPINESS OF THE PEAR.

INGREDIENTS

1 tbsp / 15 ml Refined vegetable oil
½ tsp / 2½ g Finely-chopped garlic (*lasan*)
20 pieces / 500 g Fresh water chestnuts (*singhara*), peeled
Salt to taste
¾ cup / 45 g Finely-chopped scallions (*hare pyaz ke patte*), (½ cup + ¼ cup)
1 medium / 200 g Pear (*nashpati*)
¹/₃ cup / 30 g Walnuts (*akhrot*)

For the dressing, mix and set aside:
3 tbsp / 45 ml French dressing (*Salaad-Ras Francisi*-with balsamic vinegar see p. 220)
1 tsp / 5 g Ginger (*adrak*) paste (see p. 206)
2 tsp / 10 g Mint (*pudina*) paste (see p. 207)

METHOD

• Heat the oil in a pan for 30 seconds; add the garlic and sauté on moderate heat until light brown. Add the water chestnuts and ¼ tsp salt (or to taste); continue to sauté for a minute. Add ½ cup scallions; mix and set aside.

• Just before serving, peel, core, and cut the pear into thin slices and mix with the sautéed water chestnut mixture, walnuts, and the remaining ¼ cup scallions.

• Toss lightly with the dressing on a mixing plate and serve immediately.

• Although available canned, this recipe calls for fresh water chestnuts.
• Cut the pear just before serving the salad, as it tends to discolor after it is cut.

• Balsamic vinegar is made from the freshly squeezed, unfermented juice of grapes. It has an exceptional, highly concentrated, pungent-sweet flavor and is used cautiously in dressings.

ZUCCHINI GREEN MEDLEY
Hari Bhari Zucchini Salaad

INGREDIENTS

3½ oz / 100 g Baby corn (*chotte bhutte*), cut into 1" diagonal pieces (1 cup)

2 (loosely-packed) cups Iceberg lettuce, torn by hand into 1½" pieces

1 medium / 200 g Zucchini

1 tbsp / 15 ml Refined vegetable oil

1 tbsp / 15 g White sesame seeds (*safed til*)

2 tbsp Sliced black olives (*jaitoon*)

For the dressing, mix and set aside:

1 tbsp / 15 ml Extra virgin olive oil

1 tbsp / 15 ml Balsamic vinegar (*sirka*)

2 tbsp / 30 g Ground peanuts (*moongphalli*; see p. 215)

5 Green olives, hand-pounded in a mortar and pestle

¼ tsp Garlic (*lasan*) paste (see p. 206)

⅛ tsp Ground black peppercorns (*sabut kali mirch*)

Salt to taste

METHOD

• Place the baby corn pieces and lettuce leaves in separate bowls, cover with plastic wrap, and refrigerate until chilled.

• Slit zucchini in half lengthwise and then cut breadthwise into 1½" pieces.

• Heat 1 tbsp oil in a pan for 30 seconds; add the sesame seeds. Press the zucchini pieces cut-side down on the sesame seeds in the pan.

• Fry on moderate heat for a minute or until the sesame seeds turn light brown.

• Mix the sautéed zucchini, sliced black olives, chilled baby corn, and lettuce.

• Toss with the dressing on a mixing plate, transfer to a serving dish, and serve immediately.

THE ROBUST INDO-ITALIAN FLAVORS OF THE DRESSING ENHANCE THE SUBTLE NUTTINESS OF THE SESAME-COATED ZUCCHINI AND THE CRUNCH OF THE FRESH VEGETABLES.

• Always tear lettuce leaves by hand, instead of cutting with a knife, as this helps them to stay fresh longer.

• Olive oil is obtained by pressing tree-ripened olives. Extra-virgin olive oil is considered the purest and most flavorful form and is used extensively in salads.

TANGY LETTUCE WRAP
Chatpatte Salaad Ke Paan

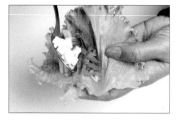

INGREDIENTS

1½ cups / 150 g Sprouted green lentils (*ankurit moong*)

8 Lettuce leaves, washed, wiped dry with a dish towel

3 oz / 75 g Carrot (*gajar*), grated (¾ cup)

¾ cup / 100 g Pickled cucumber (*khira*) (see below)

¾ cup / 90 g Paneer, cut into ¼" cubes (see p. 204)

¼ cup / 50 g Tangy-Sweet Sauce (*Tikhi-Meethi Chutney*, see p. 164)

¼ cup / 50 g Peanut Chutney (*Moongphalli Chutney*, see p. 175)

¼ cup / 50 g Sweet 'n' Sour Chutney (*Khatti-Meethi Chutney*, see p. 165)

¼ tsp White sesame seeds (*safed til*)

For the pickled cucumber, mix and set aside for 30 minutes:

3½ oz / 100 g Cucumber, deseeded, cut into thin, 1"-long pieces (¾ cup)

1 tbsp / 15 ml White vinegar (*safed sirka*)

1 tsp / 5 g Powdered sugar (see p. 217)

¼ tsp Salt

METHOD

• Boil 3¾ cups water, add the sprouts, and cook for 30 seconds; drain in a colander and set aside.

• Neatly break the stems off the lettuce and stack the leaves at one end of a large serving plate.

• Place the carrot, pickled cucumber pieces, cooked sprouts, and paneer cubes in separate bowls and arrange on the serving plate. Place each of the sauces in small bowls and sprinkle ¼ tsp white sesame seeds on the Sweet 'n' Sour Chutney. Arrange the bowls on the serving plate.

• **To eat**, take one salad leaf and apply ½ tsp of Peanut Chutney.

• Place 1 tbsp of bean sprouts, 4 pieces of pickled cucumber, 1 tsp of grated carrot, and 2 tsp of paneer cubes in the salad leaf.

• Add ½ tsp Sweet 'n' Sour Chutney and ½ tsp Tangy-Sweet Sauce.

• Fold the salad leaf and eat immediately.

• Any variety of salad greens with wide leaves may be used. However, ensure that the leaves are fresh and crisp, and show no signs of wilting.

THIS LOW-CALORIE SALAD WITH ITS FRESH MEDLEY OF FLAVORS IS A GREAT CONVERSATION STARTER ON ACCOUNT OF ITS UNIQUE SERVING STYLE.

• The Sweet 'n' Sour Chutney can be substituted for the same amount of HP or 8-to-8 sauce.

• Serve this salad with a light soup and whole-wheat toast to make a healthy meal.

LOTUS STEM & PASTA SALAD
Kamal Kakdi Pasta Salaad

INGREDIENTS

1 cup / 60 g Farfalle pasta

2 tsp / 10 ml Refined vegetable oil

1 medium / 150 g Lotus stem (*kamal kakdi*), cut into 1" diagonal pieces (see p. 209)

2 tbsp Sun-dried tomatoes

2 tbsp Black olives (*jaitoon*), thinly sliced

For the dressing: mix and set aside

2½ tbsp / 25 g Tangy-Sweet Sauce (*Tikhi-Meethi Chutney*, see p. 164)

1 tsp / 5 ml Light soy sauce

1 tbsp / 15 ml Balsamic vinegar (*sirka*)

¼ tsp Ground black peppercorns (*sabut kali mirch*)

¼ tsp Salt

For the seasoning:

1 tbsp / 15 ml Olive oil

2 tbsp / 30 g Peanuts (*moongphalli*), skinned (see p. 215)

2 Dried red chilies (*sookhi lal mirch*), broken in half

2 tbsp Basil leaves

To serve:

A handful Arugula (rocket) leaves

METHOD

- Boil 3¾ cups water; add the farfalle, and cook on low heat until firm, but not overcooked (al dente). Drain in a colander.

- Add 2 tsp oil to the drained farfalle; toss well so that the pasta doesn't stick together; set aside to cool.

- Pressure-cook the lotus stem pieces with 2 cups water to one whistle; remove from the heat and allow the pressure to drop before opening the lid. (Alternatively, cook in a soup pot until tender.) Drain in a colander and set aside (see p. 209).

- In a bowl, mix together the cooked lotus stem, farfalle, sun-dried tomatoes, and black olive rings. Add the dressing to the salad mixture and toss lightly.

- **For the seasoning,** heat the olive oil in a tempering ladle or small frying pan for 30 seconds; add the skinned peanuts and fry on low heat until light brown, stirring continuously. Add the broken dried red chilies and basil leaves; mix.

- **To serve,** arrange the arugula leaves on a flat serving dish. Arrange the dressed pasta over the arugula leaves, top with seasoning, and serve immediately.

- Farfalle pasta is shaped like a bow tie with toothed edges and is available in a variety of colors and flavors. For this recipe, use the plain, white variant.

THE ROBUST FLAVORS OF THE TANGY-SWEET DRESSING, COMBINED WITH THE UNUSUAL PAIRING OF LOTUS STEM AND FARFALLE ARE UNDERSCORED PERFECTLY BY THE CRUNCHY PEANUT SEASONING.

• Sun-drying tomatoes gives them a concentrated flavor, a chewy texture, and a deep, red color.

CRUNCHY ORIENTAL MEDLEY
Kurkuri Noodle Bhel

INGREDIENTS

½ cup / 25 g Bean sprouts

1 medium / 75 g Tomato, deseeded, cut lengthwise into 3''-strips

1 oz / 25 g Bell peppers (*Shimla mirch*), deseeded, cut into 3"-strips (¼ cup)

2 oz / 50 g Cabbage (*bandh gobi*), cut into 3"-strips (½ cup)

2 oz / 50 g Carrot (*gajar*), peeled, cut into 3"-strips (½ cup)

2 oz / 50 g Cucumber (*khira*), deseeded, cut into 3"-strips (½ cup)

1 oz / 30 g Onion, cut into long slices (2 tbsp)

3½ oz /100 g Chinese noodles

2 tsp / 10 ml Refined vegetable oil

Refined vegetable oil for deep-frying

For the dressing, mix and set aside:

1 tbsp / 15 ml White vinegar (*safed sirka*)

2 tsp / 10 g Powdered sugar (see p. 217)

2 tbsp / 30 g Tomato ketchup

¼ tsp Black peppercorns (*sabut kali mirch*), freshly ground

1 tsp / 5 ml Soy sauce

½ tsp / 2½ g Salt

½ tsp / 2½ g Red chili powder

To garnish:

A handful Lettuce leaves

2 tbsp Finely-chopped scallions (*hare pyaz ke patte*)

METHOD

• Cover the prepared vegetables with plastic wrap and refrigerate until chilled.

• Bring 5 cups water to a boil and add the noodles; cook until soft but firm.

• Strain in a colander; add 2 tsp oil and toss with a fork to prevent the noodles from sticking together.

• Pour oil to the depth of 1" in a shallow wok (*kadhai*) and heat until near-smoking point. Deep-fry the noodles on high heat, until the edges begin to turn light golden brown. Now quickly turn the noodles over to brown evenly on the other side (30-60 seconds).

• Remove, drain on paper towel, and when cool, gently break the noodles by hand and set aside.

• **To serve,** place the lettuce leaves on one side of a serving plate. Mix the fried noodles with the chilled vegetables and gently toss in the dressing.

• Place the salad mixture next to the lettuce leaves, garnish with scallions, and serve immediately.

• Heating the oil to near-smoking point ensures that the noodles turn crisp without absorbing too much oil. Flip the noodles only once to keep their nest-like shape intact, making them easier to handlle.

THE SWEET PIQUANT DRESSING COMPLEMENTS THE CHILLED VEGETABLES AND THE CRUNCHY NOODLES TO MAKE A DELECTABLE SALAD THAT CAN BE ENJOYED AS A SNACK OR MAIN COURSE.

• Add the vegetables and dressing to the fried noodles just before serving to ensure that the salad doesn't become soggy.

CHILLED MACBEAN DELIGHT
Sheetal Macrajma Bahaar

THIS CHILLED PASTA SALAD COMPLEMENTS THE WHOLESOME FLAVOR OF KIDNEY BEANS WITH THE FRESH, FRUITY TANG OF ORANGE.

INGREDIENTS

¹/₃ cup / 50 g Red kidney beans (*rajmah*)
1¼ cups / 90 g Pasta shells
2 tsp / 10 ml Refined vegetable oil
½ cup / 75 g Orange (*santra*) segments
A few Celery stalks, cut into 10 1"-pieces (see p. 211)
1 (loosely-packed) cup Arugula leaves

For the dressing, mix and set aside:
3 tbsp / 45 ml French dressing (*Salaad-Ras Francisi,* see p. 220)
1 tbsp / 15 g Tomato ketchup
½ tsp / 2½ g Chili Garlic Chutney (*Lal Lehsuni Chutney,* see p. 166)
1 tbsp / 4 g Finely-chopped fresh parsley or 1 tsp dried parsley
¼ tsp Freshly-ground black peppercorns (*sabut kali mirch*)
¼ tsp Salt

METHOD

• **For the red kidney beans,** soak the kidney beans in 3 cups water for 8 hours or overnight. Drain in a colander. Pressure cook the beans with 1½ cups water and a pinch of salt to one whistle. Simmer for 20 minutes and turn off the heat. When the pressure drops, open the lid. (Alternatively, cook in a soup pot until tender.)

• Wash under running water; drain in a colander and set aside.

• **For the pasta shells,** bring 5 cups water to a boil; add 1 tsp oil and the pasta. Bring to a boil and simmer, partially covered, until the pasta is firm but not overcooked. Drain in a colander.

• Add 1 tsp oil and toss gently to prevent the shells from sticking together.

• Place all the salad ingredients, including the cooked shells and red kidney beans in separate bowls, cover with plastic wrap, and refrigerate until chilled.

• **To serve,** mix all the chilled ingredients together on a plate and gently toss in the dressing.

• Transfer to a serving dish and serve immediately.

• Pasta shells are made from durum semolina and water.

• Arugula is also known as rocket.

• Canned red kidney beans (¾ cup) can also be used, after draining and washing.

CARAMELIZED PINEAPPLE POTATO SALAD
Bhuna Ananas Aloo Salaad

INGREDIENTS

2½ tbsp / 40 ml Refined
vegetable oil (1 tbsp + 1 tbsp +
½ tbsp)
2¼ cups / 200 g Pineapple
(*ananas*) wedges (see tip)
8 small / 200 g Potatoes, boiled,
peeled, halved lengthwise
1 medium / 65 g Yellow bell
pepper, deseeded, cut into
1" squares
A handful Lettuce leaves
1 tbsp / 4 g Finely-chopped
parsley
¼ cup / 15 g Finely-chopped
scallions (*hare pyaz ke patte*)

**For the dressing, mix and
set aside:**

1½ tbsp / 25 g Powdered
brown sugar (see p. 217)
¼ tsp Red chili flakes
¼ tsp Mustard (*sarson*) powder
2 tsp / 10 g Celery paste
(see p. 207)
1 tbsp / 15 ml Lemon juice
(*nimbu ka ras*)
2 tsp / 10 g White sesame seeds
(*safed til*), toasted, ground (see
p. 215)
½ tsp / 2½ g Salt

METHOD

• Heat 1 tbsp oil in a pan
for 30 seconds; add the
pineapple wedges and cook
on moderate heat until lightly
caramelized on both sides;
remove and set aside.

• In a separate pan, heat 1 tbsp
oil for 30 seconds; add halved
potatoes, placing them flat-
side down. Cook on moderate
heat until light brown on both
sides; remove and set aside.

• In the same pan, heat ½ tbsp
oil for 30 seconds; add the bell
pepper squares and sauté on
high heat for a minute; remove
and set aside.

• **To serve,** arrange the lettuce
leaves on a serving dish. In
a bowl, mix the sautéed
pineapple wedges, fried
potato halves, and bell pepper
squares along with the parsley
and scallions. Gently toss
in the dressing and arrange
on the salad leaves. Serve
immediately.

THIS
COMBINATION
OF HEARTY POTATOES
AND TANGY PINEAPPLE,
WITH A LIGHTLY-SPICED
BROWN SUGAR DRESSING,
CREATES AN EXCEPTIONAL
ACCOMPANIMENT TO AN
INDIAN MEAL.

• To make pineapple wedges, cut a slice of pineapple into 4-6 equal parts.

- Brown sugar is used in certain recipes for its distinctive golden-brown color and mild caramel flavor that comes from the presence of molasses.

PASTA MÉLANGE
Pasta Chaat Salaad

INGREDIENTS

¼ lb / 100 g Fettuccine
2 tsp / 10 ml Refined vegetable oil
2 tbsp / 30 g Cornstarch
Refined vegetable oil for deep-frying
3 medium / 225 g Potatoes, peeled, cut into fingers, immersed in water
2 oz / 50 g Yellow bell pepper, cut into 3"-thin strips (½ cup)
2 oz / 50 g Red bell pepper, cut into 3"-thin strips (½ cup)
2 oz / 50 g Green bell pepper (*Shimla mirch*), cut into 3''-thin strips (½ cup)

For the dressing, mix and set aside:

1½ tbsp / 25 g Sweet 'n' Sour Chutney (*Khatti-Meethi Chutney*, see p. 165)
1 tsp / 5 g Chili Garlic Chutney (*Lal Lehsuni Chutney*, see p. 166)
1 tbsp / 15 ml White vinegar (*safed sirka*)
2 tbsp / 30 g Tomato ketchup
¼ cup / 15 g Finely-chopped scallions (*hare pyaz ke patte*)
1 tbsp / 4 g Finely-chopped cilantro (*dhaniya*) leaves
1 tsp / 5 g Powdered sugar (see p. 217)
1 tsp / 5 g Garlic (*lasan*) paste (see p. 206)
½ tsp / 2½ g Green chili paste (see p. 206)
¼ tsp Black peppercorns (*sabut kali mirch*), freshly ground
Salt to taste

To garnish:

2 tsp / 10 g White sesame seeds (*safed til*), toasted (see p. 215)
2 tbsp / 8 g Finely-chopped scallions (*hare pyaz ke patte*)
1 tbsp / 4 g Finely-chopped cilantro (*dhaniya*) leaves
A handful Lettuce leaves

METHOD

- Bring 5 cups water to a boil and add the fettuccine. Cover, turn off the heat, and let the pasta stand for 5-8 minutes. Test the pasta by pressing between your fore finger and thumb; it should feel firm but not overcooked (al dente).

- Drain in a colander. Add 2 tsp oil to the drained fettuccine and toss well so the pasta doesn't stick together; set aside to cool.

- Transfer the fettuccine to a flat dish; sprinkle 2 tbsp cornstarch on the fettuccine and toss lightly to coat evenly.

- Pour oil to the depth of 1'' in a shallow wok (*kadhai*) and heat. Deep-fry the potato fingers on moderately high heat until light golden-brown; remove, drain on an absorbent paper towel and set aside.

- Deep-fry the fettuccine in the same oil, in small batches, on high heat, until golden in color; remove, drain on an absorbent paper towel, and set aside.

- When cool, gently separate the fettuccine ribbons by hand.

- **To serve,** reserve a few strips of each of the bell peppers and fried potato fingers to use as garnish. Just before serving, mix the rest of the fried fettuccine, potato fingers, and bell pepper strips; add the dressing and toss lightly.

- Arrange the salad mixture on a serving plate. Sprinkle toasted sesame seeds, scallions, and cilantro leaves. Garnish with lettuce leaves, reserved potato fingers, and bell pepper strips. Serve immediately.

THE CRISPY MÉLANGE OF FETTUCCINE, FRIED POTATOES, AND BELL PEPPERS TOSSED IN A HOT AND SWEET DRESSING MAKES FOR A DELICIOUSLY UNUSUAL, ANYTIME SALAD.

- In Italian, fettuccine translates to "little ribbons," as their appearance is long, flat, and almost ribbon-like.

• The Sweet 'n' Sour Chutney can be substituted with 2 tsp of 8-to-8 or HP sauce.
  Store-bought red chili sauce may be used instead of the Chili Garlic Chutney.

SNACKS & APPETIZERS

BREAKFAST ENERGY BOWL
Daliya Savera

INGREDIENTS
1 tsp / 5 g Clarified butter (*ghee*)
¾ cup / 125 g Bulgar / cracked wheat (*daliya*)
4 tbsp / 60 g Sugar
2 cups / 400 ml Milk
1½ tbsp / 25 g Raisins (*kishmish*)

To garnish:
2 tbsp / 20 g Almonds (*badam*), peeled (see p. 218)
1 tbsp / 10 g Pistachios (*pista*), peeled (see p. 218)

METHOD
- Heat 1 tsp clarified butter in a wok (*kadhai*) for 30 seconds; add the bulgar and cook on low heat, stirring frequently until evenly light golden brown. Remove and set aside (see p. 215). Pressure-cook the toasted bulgar with 2 cups / 475 ml water to one whistle and turn off the heat and allow the pressure to drop before removing the lid. (Alternatively, cook in a saucepan until tender.)

- Add the sugar and milk.

- Turn the heat back on and add the raisins. Bring the mixture to a boil and simmer for 10 minutes.

- Serve hot, garnished with almonds and pistachios.

BULGAR
IS A HEALTHY CEREAL,
USUALLY SERVED AT BREAKFAST
TIME IN INDIA. BEING A COMPLEX
CARBOHYDRATE, IT PROVIDES AN
INVIGORATING START TO A
BUSY DAY.

- Since cooked bulgar tends to absorb milk and thicken, when serving, add more milk, if required.

- The calorie conscious can use skim or low-fat milk and omit the dried fruits and nuts.

SAVORY BOWL 'O' HEALTH
Daliya Hara Bhara

INGREDIENTS

1 tsp / 5 g Clarified butter (*ghee*)

1 cup / 170 g Bulgar / cracked wheat (*daliya*)

¼ lb / 125 g Broccoli, cut into ½" florets

A pinch Sugar

1½ tbsp / 25 ml Refined vegetable oil

2 medium / 150 g Onions, cut into medium-size cubes

15 Curry leaves (*kadhi patta*)

1 tsp / 5 g Ginger (*adrak*) paste (see p. 206)

¼ tsp Green chili paste (see p. 206)

2 medium / 150 g Tomatoes, cut into medium-size cubes

$1/_8$ tsp Turmeric (*haldi*) powder

¼ tsp Red chili powder

Salt to taste

½ cup / 75 g Shelled peas (*hara mattar*), cooked (see p. 210)

2 tbsp / 8 g Finely-chopped cilantro (*dhaniya*) leaves

PACKED WITH THE GOODNESS OF VEGETABLES, THIS SAVORY SNACK ALSO MAKES FOR A COMPLETE AND NUTRITIOUS ONE-DISH MEAL.

METHOD

- Heat 1 tsp clarified butter in a wok (*kadhai*) for 30 seconds; add the bulgar and cook on low heat, stirring frequently until evenly light golden brown. Remove and set aside (see p. 215).

- Bring 2½ cups / 600 ml water to a boil; add the broccoli florets with a pinch of sugar and cook for 2 minutes; drain in a colander and set aside.

- Heat 1½ tbsp oil in a pan for 30 seconds; add the onion cubes, curry leaves, and ginger and green chili pastes and sauté on moderate heat for a minute.

- Add the tomatoes and cook for 30 seconds; add the turmeric and red chili powders and mix. Add the toasted bulgar, 2 cups / 475 ml water, and salt to taste. Bring the mixture to a boil and cook, covered, on low heat until the water evaporates, stirring occasionally. Uncover the pan, add the cooked broccoli, peas, and cilantro leaves; mix and serve hot.

- Add the cooked broccoli florets and peas just before serving otherwise they tend to discolor.

- Bulgar / cracked wheat is obtained by crushing whole wheat. It is a rich source of vitamins and minerals. It is easily available in supermarkets.

NUTTY SAGO PEARLS
Saboo Dana Khichidi

INGREDIENTS

¾ cup / 125 g Sago
(*saboo dana*)
2 tbsp / 30 ml Refined
vegetable oil
½ tsp / 2½ g Mustard seeds
(*rai*)
8 Curry leaves (*kadhi patta*)
1 tsp / 5 g Chopped ginger
(*adrak*)
1 Green chili, slit
¹/₃ cup / 75 g Skinned peanuts
(*moongphalli*, see p. 215)
2 medium / 150 g Potatoes,
boiled, peeled (see p. 208), cut
into medium-sized cubes
Salt to taste
2 tbsp / 8 g Finely-chopped
cilantro (*dhaniya*) leaves
1 tsp / 5 ml Lemon juice
(*nimbu ka ras*)

METHOD

• Wash and drain the sago. Place in a flat vessel and pour water exactly up to the level of the sago (adding too much water will make it sticky and spoil the texture); leave covered for 3-4 hours. To check if the sago is ready to be used, press a few pearls between your thumb and forefinger; they should feel soft, but firm.

• Heat 2 tbsp oil in a pan for 30 seconds; add the mustard seeds. When they splutter, add the curry leaves, ginger, and green chili; mix. Add the skinned peanuts and sauté on moderate heat for 30 seconds.

• Now add the potato cubes and cook for 30 seconds. Lower the heat and add the soaked sago, salt to taste, cilantro leaves, and lemon juice.

• Mix gently for 1-2 minutes on high heat and serve immediately.

> THIS IS A VARIATION OF A TRADITIONAL DISH THAT IS EATEN IN NORTHERN INDIA DURING NAVARATHRI, A FESTIVAL HONORING GODDESS DURGA.

• Sago is soaked before cooking to rehydrate it. Depending on its quality, it may need to be soaked for anywhere between 2-8 hours.

• When this dish is made during fasting rituals in India, cumin seeds are used in place of mustard seeds.

SPICY SWEET CORN PATTIES
Chatpati Makai Tikkia

INGREDIENTS

6 medium / 450 g Potatoes, boiled, peeled, grated (see p. 208)

¼ tsp Red chili powder

½ tsp / 2½ g Salt

Refined vegetable oil for deep-frying

For the filling, mix and set aside:

½ cup / 75 g canned corn (*makai*) kernels

½ tsp / 2½ g Red chili powder

1 tbsp / 4 g Finely-chopped cilantro (*dhaniya*) leaves

½ tsp / 2½ g Finely-chopped green chilies

½ tsp / 2½ g Dried mango powder (*amchur*)

½ tsp / 2½ g *Garam masala* powder (see p. 214)

For the coating, mix and set aside:

2 heaped tbsp / 40 g Cornstarch

2 heaped tbsp / 40 g All-purpose flour (*maida*)

To serve:

½ cup Green Coconut Chutney (*Hari Nariyal Chutney*, see p. 171)

METHOD

- Mix the grated potatoes with red chili powder and salt; knead gently into a smooth mixture and divide into 12 equal balls.

- Flatten each potato ball on your palm, place 1 tsp of the corn filling in the center, fold, and shape into a flat, round patty.

- Coat each patty evenly with the flour mixture and press lightly between your palms to bind.

- Pour oil to a depth of 1" in a wok (*kadhai*) and heat to smoking point. Deep-fry the patties, 4 at a time, in hot oil until light golden brown. Remove and drain on a paper towel.

- Serve hot, accompanied with Green Coconut Chutney.

THE NATURAL SWEETNESS OF THE CORN WITH THE CRUNCHY POTATO CASING PAIRS PERFECTLY WITH THE SLIGHTLY SPICY, GREEN COCONUT CHUTNEY.

- Kernels from the fresh corn on the cob (*desi butta*) can be substituted for the canned corn in this recipe.

- Corn on the cob must be first cooked with sufficient water and 1 tsp sugar. Drain and remove the kernels.

STUFFED LENTIL PANCAKES
Bhare Hare Cheele

INGREDIENTS

½ cup / 100 g Whole green gram lentils (*sabut moong dal*)
½ cup / 100 g Split green gram lentils (*chilka moong dal*)
¼ cup / 50 g Rice
2 tsp / 10 g Chopped green chilies
¼ tsp Baking powder
Salt to taste
Refined vegetable oil for cooking

For the filling:
1 tsp / 5 g Husked split black gram (*dhuli urad dal*)
1 tsp / 5 g Husked split Bengal gram (*chana dal*)
2 tbsp / 30 ml Refined vegetable oil
½ tsp / 2½ g Mustard seeds (*rai*)
10 Curry leaves (*kadhi patta*)
2 medium / 150 g Onions, cut into long slices
1 tsp / 5 g Finely-chopped green chilies
¼ tsp Turmeric (*haldi*) powder
3 medium / 225 g Potatoes, boiled (see p. 208), peeled, broken into small pieces
1 tbsp / 4 g Finely-chopped cilantro (*dhaniya*) leaves

To serve:
1¼ cups Coconut Chutney (*Nariyal Chutney*, see p. 174)

METHOD

- Wash and soak the whole green gram, split green gram, and raw rice together for 4 hours in plenty of water; drain in a colander.

- In a blender / food processor, coarsely grind the lentils, rice, and green chilies with water to a medium-consistency batter.

- Transfer the batter to a vessel; add the baking powder and salt to taste; mix and set aside for 1 hour.

- **For the filling,** wash and soak the husked, split black gram and Bengal gram together for 5 minutes; drain in a colander and set aside. Heat 2 tbsp oil in a pan for 30 seconds; add the mustard seeds. When they splutter, add the soaked lentils and sauté on moderate heat until light golden brown. Add the curry leaves, onion slices, and green chilies; fry until the onions turn light brown, stirring continuously.

- Add the turmeric powder and boiled potato pieces; mix.

- Add salt to taste and cilantro leaves; cook for 2 minutes, stirring occasionally; set aside.

- **For the pancakes,** heat a nonstick pan and brush with oil; add 1½ tbsp batter and spread with a spoon until 6" wide.

- Drizzle 2 tsp oil around the sides of the pancake and fry on moderate heat until light golden brown. Flip the pancake, cook for 30 seconds, and flip again.

- Place 1½ tbsp of the potato filling in the center of the pancake, fold, and serve hot, accompanied with Coconut Chutney.

- Wipe the pan with a moist cloth before spreading each pancake.

- Avoid using brown rice, as it will alter the color and texture of this dish.

A SPECIALTY OF THE SOUTHERN STATE OF ANDHRA PRADESH, THIS DISH IS A DELICIOUS COUSIN OF THE UBIQUITOUS MASALA DOSA AND IS LOCALLY KNOWN AS PESARATTU.

• Make sure that the batter is neither too fine, nor too coarse, so that the pancake texture has the necessary, slight crunch.

KEBAB 'O' LENTIL
Dal Ke Kebab

INGREDIENTS

1 cup / 150 g Black chickpeas (*kala chana*), washed, soaked in 4 cups water for 8 hours or overnight, drained
⅓ cup / 50 g Skinned, split Bengal gram (*chana dal*), washed, soaked in 4 cups water for 2 hours, drained
1 medium / 75 g Potato, boiled, peeled, grated (see p. 208)
8 Slices bread, dipped in water, squeezed (see p. 216)
2 tsp / 10 g Ginger (*adrak*) paste (see p. 206)
2 tsp / 10 g Garlic (*lasan*) paste (see p. 206)
1 tsp / 5 g Green chili paste (see p. 206)
2 tbsp / 8 g Finely-chopped mint (*pudina*) leaves
Salt to taste
Refined vegetable oil for shallow-frying

To serve:
Pickled Onions (*Pyaz Sirkewale*, see p. 173)
Mint Yogurt Chutney (*Pudina Dahi Chutney*, see p. 172)

METHOD

- Pressure cook the black chickpeas with 2 cups water and a pinch of salt to one whistle; simmer for 30 minutes and turn off the heat. Let the pressure drop before removing the lid. (Alternatively, cook in a soup pot until tender.) Drain in a colander.

- Boil 2½ cups water in a pan, add the soaked, split Bengal gram and simmer on low heat until cooked (soft but firm); drain in a colander.

- Coarsely mash the cooked black chickpeas and husked split Bengal gram separately with a stone grinder (*sil-batta*) or rolling pin; transfer both to a large plate.

- Add the grated potatoes, squeezed bread, ginger, garlic and green chili pastes, mint leaves, and salt to taste; mix well.

- Divide the mixture into equal portions and shape into round, flat kebabs, 2" in diameter.

- Pour oil to the depth of ¼" in a flat pan and heat until near smoking point. Add 2-4 kebabs, at intervals, and with a slotted spoon, drizzle hot oil from the pan on top of the kebabs, until the sides begin to turn light golden brown. Now flip and shallow-fry until evenly brown on the other side. Remove and drain on an absorbent paper towel. Repeat the process to fry the remaining kebabs.

- Serve hot, accompanied with Pickled Onions and Mint Yogurt Chutney.

THIS DISH IS A DELICIOUS VEGETARIAN VARIATION OF THE MEAT KEBAB, AND MAKES AN EXCELLENT APPETIZER OR COCKTAIL SNACK.

- The water used to cook the black chickpeas may be reserved and used as a base to prepare a nutritious soup or drink.

- Keep the temperature of the oil at near-smoking point while frying the kebabs; otherwise they may break.

- Roll 1-2 kebabs up in a Handkerchief Fold (see p. 140) with Pickled Onions (see p. 173) to make a delicious wrap.

SPICY GRAM FLOUR ROLLS
Khandvi

INGREDIENTS

Refined vegetable oil
for greasing
1 cup / 200 g Sour yogurt (*dahi*),
set to a firm consistency
1 cup / 100 g Gram flour
(*besan*)
½ tsp / 2½ g Turmeric (*haldi*)
powder
⅛ tsp Asafoetida (*hing*)
2 tsp / 10 g Ginger (*adrak*) paste
(see p. 206)
2 tsp / 10 g Green chili paste
(see p. 206)
Salt to taste

For the tempering:
1 tbsp / 15 ml Refined
vegetable oil
1 tsp / 5 g Mustard seeds (*rai*)
A pinch Asafoetida
1 tbsp Chopped curry leaves
(*kadhi patta*)

To garnish:
3 tbsp / 12 g Finely-chopped
cilantro (*dhaniya*) leaves
2 tbsp / 30 g Grated fresh
coconut (*nariyal*, see p. 210)
½ cup Green Coconut Chutney
(*Hari Nariyal Chutney*, see p. 171)

METHOD

- Lightly grease the underside of 6 large steel plates (*thalis*) about 12" in diameter with oil and set aside.

- In a large bowl, combine the yogurt, gram flour, 2 cups / 475 ml water, turmeric powder, asafoetida, ginger and green chili pastes, and salt to taste and whisk to a smooth consistency.

- Place this mixture in a wok (*kadhai*) and cook on moderate heat, stirring continuously to avoid lumps forming.

- Once it thickens, test the consistency of one teaspoon of the mixture by spreading a thin layer on a greased plate. If you can lift the thin strip off the plate without it breaking, you have achieved the right texture. If not, continue cooking and testing the mixture.

- Using a flat spatula, quickly spread 2 heaped tbsp of the mixture onto each greased steel plate as fast as possible, while the mixture is still hot.

- Using a pizza cutter or knife, cut the sheets into 1¼"-broad strips and roll each strip gently with your fingers, making 1"-thick rolls. Arrange the rolls (*kandvi*) on a serving plate.

- **For the tempering,** heat 1 tbsp oil in a tempering ladle for 30 seconds; add the mustard seeds and when they splutter, add asafoetida and curry leaves. Pour the tempering uniformly over the rolls.

- Garnish with cilantro leaves and coconut. Serve at room temperature accompanied with Green Coconut Chutney.

- Yogurt that has been kept refrigerated for two days is ideal for this recipe.

- Cooked gram flour batter tends to solidify as it cools. Make sure you spread it on the greased plate as quickly as you can.

A SPECIALTY OF WESTERN INDIA, THIS IS A LIGHT, DELICATELY SPICED DISH, EMBELLISHED WITH THE COMBINED FLAVORS OF COCONUT, CILANTRO, AND MUSTARD SEEDS.

• Refrigerate any leftover rolls and consume within 24 hours, as this dish tends to ferment.

INDIAN BURGER
Vada Paav

INGREDIENTS

12 *Paavs* (see tip)
1½ tbsp Garlic relish
1½ tbsp / 25 g Butter, at room temperature
½ cup Sweet 'n' Sour Chutney (*Khatti-Meethi Chutney*, see p. 165)
½ cup Garlic Green Chutney (*Lehsuni Hari Chutney*, see p. 170)
12 *Vadas* (see recipe below)

For the garlic relish:
1 tbsp / 15 ml Refined vegetable oil
15 Garlic (*lasan*) cloves
2 tsp / 10 g Red chili powder
¼ tsp Salt

For the *vadas*:
Refined vegetable oil for cooking and deep-frying
½ tsp / 2½ g Mustard seeds (*rai*)
8 Curry leaves (*kadhi patta*), chopped
½ tsp / 2½ g Garlic paste (see p. 206)
¼ tsp Turmeric (*haldi*) powder
5 medium / 375 g Potatoes, boiled, peeled, coarsely mashed (see p. 208)
½ tsp / 2½ g Chopped green chilies
2 tbsp / 8 g Chopped cilantro (*dhaniya*) leaves
Salt to taste

For the batter:
1 cup / 100 g Gram flour (*besan*)
¼ tsp Baking powder
Salt to taste

METHOD

- **For the garlic relish**, heat 1 tbsp oil in a pan for 30 seconds; add the garlic cloves and sauté on moderate heat for 10 seconds. Add the red chili powder and salt; mix well. Turn off the heat and cool.

- Pound the mixture in a mortar and pestle until smooth; set aside.

- **For the *vadas***, heat 1 tbsp oil in a pan for 30 seconds; add the mustard seeds and when they splutter, add the curry leaves, garlic paste, and turmeric powder. Add the mashed potatoes and mix well. Add the green chilies and cilantro, season with salt to taste, and cook for 2 minutes on moderate heat, stirring occasionally; set aside to cool.

- Divide the mixture into 12 equal balls.

- **For the batter**: Prepare a semi-thick batter with the gram flour, baking powder, salt, and approximately ½ cup / 100 ml water. Pour oil to the depth of 1" in a wok (*kadhai*) and heat until moderately hot. Dip each potato ball into the batter, ensuring it is evenly coated.

- Deep-fry the balls (*vadas*) in batches of 4-6, in moderately hot oil, until evenly light golden brown. Remove and drain on a paper towel.

- **To serve**, slit each *paav* horizontally into two. On one half apply 1 tsp of garlic relish and on the other half apply ½ tsp of butter. Pan-toast both halves, face down, in a nonstick pan, until light golden brown.

- Apply 2 tsp of Sweet 'n' Sour Chutney to the half with the garlic relish and 2 tsp of Garlic Green Chutney to the buttered half.

- Sandwich a *vada* between the two halves, press firmly, and serve.

- *Paavs* are a kind of small, soft, square-shaped bun, available in India. They are also found in specialty Indian stores. If *paavs* are not available, use normal, soft, round buns.

VADA
PAAV IS A POPULAR
STREET FOOD SPECIALTY
IN WESTERN INDIA, AND IS
OFTEN EATEN AS A
SATISFYING, QUICK
MEAL ON THE
GO.

• The *vadas* may be prepared 1-2 hours ahead of serving.

SAUTÉED WATER CHESTNUTS
Garma Garam Singhade

INGREDIENTS

1-2 tbsp / 15-20 ml Refined vegetable oil

¼ cup / 40 g Cooked or canned corn (*makai*) kernels

1 tsp / 5 g Finely-chopped garlic (*lasan*)

1 tsp / 5 g Finely-chopped ginger (*adrak*)

1 slightly-heaped tbsp / 15 g Gram flour (*besan*)

25 Fresh water chestnuts (*singhada*), peeled

¼ tsp Red chili powder

¼ tsp Black peppercorns (*sabut kali mirch*), freshly ground

Salt to taste

½ tsp / 2½ g *Chaat masala* (see p. 214)

1 tbsp / 4 g Chopped mint (*pudina*) leaves

4 tbsp / 24 g Finely-chopped scallions (*hare pyaz ke patte*), (2 tbsp + 2 tbsp)

METHOD

• Heat 1 tsp oil in a pan for 30 seconds; add the corn kernels and sauté on moderate heat for 30 seconds; set aside.

• In a separate pan, heat 1½ tbsp oil for 30 seconds; add the garlic, ginger, and gram flour; cook on moderate heat for 20 seconds. Add the water chestnuts and mix.

• Add the red chili powder, freshly ground black pepper, and salt to taste; mix and sauté on high heat for 2 minutes, stirring frequently. Add the *chaat masala,* mint leaves, and 2 tbsp scallions; mix.

• Serve hot along with the sautéed sweet corn, garnished with the remaining 2 tbsp scallions.

THE SURPRISE ELEMENT OF THIS RECIPE IS THE HUMBLE TOASTED GRAM FLOUR, WHICH GIVES THIS DISH A WARM, TOASTY FLAVOR AND AROMA.

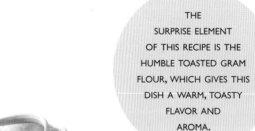

• This recipe calls for tender water chestnuts; avoid the ones that are hard to peel.

• For an added zing, sauté the water chestnuts in mustard oil instead of vegetable oil.

NUTTY PANEER
Mazeedaar Makai Paneer

FLAVORED WITH PEANUT SAUCE AND GARNISHED WITH CORN, THIS DISH IS A QUICK, NOUVELLE CUISINE VERSION OF THE TRADITIONAL INDIAN PANEER TIKKA.

INGREDIENTS
¾ cup / 115 g Cooked or canned corn (*makai*) kernels
Salt to taste
1 tsp / 5 g Ginger (*adrak*) paste (see p. 206)
¾ lb / 400 g Paneer, cut into 1" cubes (see p. 204)
2 tbsp / 8 g Finely-chopped cilantro (*dhaniya*) leaves
½ cup Peanut Chutney (*Moongphalli Chutney*, see p. 175)
Refined vegetable oil for cooking

To garnish:
½ cup / 30 g Finely-chopped scallions (*hare pyaz ke patte*)

METHOD
- **For the corn,** heat 2 tsp oil in a pan for 30 seconds; add the sweet corn kernels and salt to taste. Cook for a minute on moderate heat; set aside.

- **For the paneer,** heat 1½ tbsp oil in a pan for 30 seconds; add the ginger paste and paneer, mix. Add the cilantro leaves and salt to taste. Mix and sauté on high heat for 2 minutes, stirring continuously; set aside.

- **To serve,** arrange the sautéed paneer pieces on a serving plate and pour the peanut chutney evenly over the pieces. Garnish with scallions and sautéed sweet corn kernels; serve hot.

- If using packaged paneer, immerse the cubes in lukewarm water with a pinch of salt for 15 minutes, before sautéing, to enhance their softness.

HINT 'O' MINT CHEESE TIKKA
Pudina Paneer Tikka

INGREDIENTS

1 lb / 500 g Paneer, cut into 1" cubes (see p. 204)
½ lb / 250 g Broccoli, cut into 1" florets
Refined vegetable oil for cooking
1 large / 200 g Yellow bell pepper, cut into 1" slanted pieces
Chaat masala to taste (see p. 214)

For the marinade, mix and set aside:
½ cup / 100 g Yogurt cheese (hung yogurt; chakka; see p. 202)
2 tsp / 10 g Ginger (adrak) paste (see p. 206)
2 tsp / 10 g Garlic (lasan) paste (see p. 206)
2 tsp / 10 g Green chili paste (see p. 206)
1 tbsp / 15 g Mint (pudina) paste (see p. 207)
½ tsp / 2½ g Black peppercorns (sabut kali mirch), freshly ground
¼ tsp Garam masala powder (see p. 214)
¼ tsp Lemon juice (nimbu ka ras)
2 tbsp / 30 g Ground peanuts (moongphalli; see p. 215)
Salt to taste

To serve:
½ cup Yogurt Mustard Dip (Dahi-Rai Chutney, see p. 168)

METHOD

- Gently coat the paneer cubes with the marinade, cover with plastic wrap, and refrigerate for 1 hour.

- Bring 3¾ cups water to a boil, add the broccoli florets, and cook for 2 minutes; drain in a colander and set aside.

- Heat 2 tsp oil for 30 seconds in a nonstick pan; add the bell pepper pieces and sauté on high heat for 30 seconds. Season with salt to taste; remove and set aside.

- In a separate pan, heat 1 tbsp oil for 30 seconds; add the boiled broccoli florets and sauté on high heat for a minute. Season with salt to taste; remove and set aside.

- Heat 1 tbsp oil in a nonstick pan for 30 seconds; pick out 10-12 marinated paneer cubes and add to the pan. Cook on high heat, tossing frequently until light brown on all sides. Sprinkle chaat masala to taste; remove.

- Sauté the remaining paneer pieces in batches, adding 1 tbsp oil before each batch.

- Place the sautéed paneer cubes, broccoli florets, and bell pepper on a flat plate and serve hot, accompanied with Yogurt Mustard Dip .

THE SURPRISING MÉLANGE OF FRESH MINT AND GROUND PEANUTS GIVES THIS DISH ITS UNUSUAL AND SUBTLE PEPPERY-NUTTY FLAVOR.

- You may use the same nonstick pan for sautéing the vegetables and paneer. Make sure to rinse and wipe the pan before each use.

- Don't add the leftover marinade when sautéing the paneer, as it can alter the texture. However, the leftover marinade makes for a great homemade spread.

CHEESE TIKKA À LA SAFFRON
Zafrani Paneer Tikka

INGREDIENTS

¼ tsp Saffron (*kesar*)

1 tsp / 5 ml Milk, hot

1 kg Paneer (see p. *204*), cut into 1" cubes

Refined vegetable oil for cooking

2 large / 200 g Onions, cut into 1" pieces (see tip)

½ lb / 250 g Green bell peppers (*Shimla mirch*), deseeded, cut into 1" pieces

3 large / 300 g Tomatoes, deseeded, cut into 1" pieces

Chaat masala (see p. *214*) to taste

For the tandoori masala, mix together and set aside:

1 cup / 200 g Yogurt cheese (hung yogurt; *chakka*; see p. 202)

2 tsp / 10 g Ginger (*adrak*) paste (see p. 206)

2 tsp / 10 g Garlic (*lasan*) paste (see p. 206)

1 tsp / 5 g *Garam masala* powder (see p. 214)

1 tsp / 5 g Red chili powder

¼ tsp Lemon juice (*nimbu ka ras*)

2 tsp / 10 g Cumin (*jeera*) seeds

Salt to taste

To serve:

Pickled Onions (*Pyaz Sirkewale*, see p. 173)

Mint Yogurt Chutney (*Pudina Dahi Chutney*, see p. 172)

SAFFRON ADDS A FESTIVE TOUCH TO THIS CLASSIC INDIAN APPETIZER, ENJOYED FOR ITS ROBUST FLAVORS AND MEDLEY OF TEXTURES.

METHOD

- Soak the saffron in hot milk for 2 minutes; crush the mixture well in a mortar and pestle and mix with the tandoori masala mixture.

- Gently apply the masala marinade over the paneer cubes, cover with plastic wrap, and refrigerate for 1 hour.

- Heat 2 tbsp oil in a nonstick pan for 30 seconds; add the onions, season with salt to taste, and sauté on high heat for a minute; remove and set aside. In the same pan, heat 2 tbsp oil for 30 seconds; add the pepper, season with salt to taste, and sauté on high heat for 30 seconds; remove and set aside. In a similar manner, sauté the tomatoes, season with salt to taste; remove and set aside.

- In a separate nonstick pan, heat 1-2 tbsp oil for 30 seconds and sauté 8-10 marinated paneer pieces on moderate heat, turning frequently until evenly brown. Remove and sprinkle *chaat masala* to taste.

- Sauté the remaining paneer pieces in batches, adding 1 tbsp oil before each batch.

- Skewer a few sautéed vegetables and paneer pieces on toothpicks or long skewers and serve hot, accompanied with Pickled Onions and Mint Yogurt Chutney.

- For the onion pieces, first cut each onion into four parts and separate the layers beginning with the outermost one. Cut each layer into 1" pieces.

• The paneer may be marinated for up to 8 hours.

• Instead of sautéing the marinated paneer cubes, they can be brushed with oil and cooked on a grill or barbecue.

BROCCOLI CHEESE KEBABS
Hare Paneer Kebab

INGREDIENTS

½ lb / 250 g Broccoli, cut into
1½" florets (see tip)
¼ lb /125 g Paneer (see p. 204),
grated
2 Bread slices, dipped in water,
squeezed (see p. 216)
2 tsp / 10 g Celery paste
(see p. 207)
2 tsp / 10 g Parsley paste
(see p. 207)
½ tsp / 2½ g Freshly-ground
black peppercorns (*sabut kali
mirch*)
Salt to taste
Refined vegetable oil for frying

To serve:

½ cup Date Yogurt Dip
(*Khajoori Dahi Chutney*,
see p. 169)

METHOD

- Boil 3¾ cups water, add the broccoli florets, and cook for 2 minutes.

- Drain in a colander, cool, grate, and set aside.

- Mix the grated broccoli and paneer with squeezed bread slices, celery and parsley pastes, freshly ground black pepper, and salt to taste.

- Divide this mixture into 10-12 equal portions; shape into round, flat patties and set aside.

- Pour oil to the depth of ¼" in a shallow pan and heat until hot. Add 3-4 patties and at intervals, using a slotted spoon, drizzle hot oil from the pan on top of the patties until the sides begin to turn light golden brown.

- Flip and fry until evenly brown on the other side. Remove and drain on a paper towel. Serve hot, accompanied with Date Yogurt Dip. Repeat the process to shallow-fry the remaining patties and serve as above.

THIS
DELICATELY
SPICED KEBAB HAS AN
UNUSUAL GOLDEN-GREEN
COLOR THAT ADDS A VISUALLY
PLEASING DIMENSION TO THIS
DELICIOUS HORS D'OEUVRE.

- Adding squeezed, moist bread helps to bind all the ingredients of the patty mixture.

- The weight of the broccoli florets should be 6 oz / 175 g.

• When shallow-frying the patties, flip them only once, as they are delicate and can break if over-handled.

GREEN FLORET FRITTERS
Hare Pakode Tilwale

INGREDIENTS

20 Broccoli florets, 1" in size
2 tbsp / 30 g White sesame seeds (safed til)
Refined vegetable oil for deep-frying

For the batter:
4 heaped tbsp / 80 g All-purpose flour (maida)
4 heaped tbsp / 80 g Cornstarch
2 tsp / 10 ml Milk
¼ tsp Baking powder
½ tsp / 2½ g Freshly-ground black peppercorns (sabut kali mirch)
1 tsp / 5 g Celery paste (see p. 207)
1 tsp / 5 g Parsley paste (see p. 207)
Salt to taste

To serve:
¼ cup Peanut Chutney (Moongphalli Chutney, see p. 175)
¼ cup Tangy-Sweet Sauce (Tikhi-Meethi Chutney, see p. 164)

METHOD

• **For the batter,** mix the all-purpose flour with cornstarch, milk, baking powder, freshly ground black pepper, celery and parsley pastes, salt to taste, and approximately ¼ cup / 50 ml water, until you have a semi-thick batter; set aside.

• Bring 3¾ cups water to a boil, add the broccoli florets, and cook for 30 seconds; drain in a colander and set aside.

• Sprinkle the white sesame seeds on a plate. Dip each broccoli floret into the batter and squeeze gently to remove any excess batter. Press each batter-coated floret on the sesame seeds.

• Pour oil to the depth of 1" into a wok (kadhai) and heat until moderately hot. Deep-fry the coated florets in moderately-hot oil until light golden-brown.

• Remove and drain on a paper towel. Serve hot, accompanied with Peanut Chutney and Tangy-Sweet Sauce.

PAIRED WITH
A COMBINATION OF
NUTTY AND LEMONY SAUCES,
THE CRUNCHY SESAME-COATED
BROCCOLI IS A DELICIOUS
AND EASY-TO-MAKE
PARTY SNACK.

• Always choose broccoli with deep green florets; this indicates its freshness.

- Follow the boiling time for the broccoli florets, as over-cooking will alter their texture.

LOTUS STEM SANDWICH FRITTERS
Kamal Kakdi Sandwich Kurkure

INGREDIENTS

1 medium / 150 g Lotus stem
(*kamal kakdi*), cut into 24,
slanted pieces
2 large / 200 g Potatoes, boiled,
peeled, grated (see p. 208)
1 tsp Finely-chopped celery
(see p. 211)
1 tsp Finely-chopped parsley
½ tsp / 2½ g Green chili paste
(see p. 206)
Salt to taste
Refined vegetable oil for
deep-frying

For the batter:

2 heaped tbsp / 40 g
Cornstarch
2 heaped tbsp / 40 g
All-purpose flour (*maida*)
1 tsp / 5 g Gram flour (*besan*)
¼ tsp Baking powder
2 tsp / 10 ml Milk
Salt to taste

To serve:

½ cup Tangy-Sweet Sauce
(*Tikhi-Meethi Chutney*, see p. 164)

METHOD

- **For the batter**, prepare a semi-thick batter with cornstarch, all-purpose and gram flours, baking powder, milk, salt to taste, and enough water to make a semi-thick batter.

- Boil 3¾ cups water; add the lotus stem pieces and cook on moderate heat for 5 minutes; drain in a colander and set aside.

- Mix the grated potatoes, celery, parsley, green chili paste, and salt to taste. Divide the mixture into 12 equal balls and set aside.

- Take two lotus stem pieces and sandwich one potato ball between them.

- Pat the sandwiched potato mixture inwards gently to prevent excess spilling out. Repeat to make 12 sandwiches.

- Pour oil to the depth of 1" in a heavy-bottomed pan or wok (*kadhai*) and heat until moderately hot. Dip each sandwich in the batter, remove, place on a plate, and with your finger, gently level out any excess batter.

- Deep-fry in batches of 4-6 in moderately-hot oil, until light golden brown. Remove and drain on a paper towel.

- Serve hot, accompanied with Tangy-Sweet Sauce.

- Lotus stems are available in various sizes; for this dish, select the ones that are at least 1½" in diameter.

THE
CRUNCHY,
DELICATE COMBINATION OF
LOTUS STEM AND POTATO
IS PERFECTLY COMPLEMENTED BY
THE TANGY, SWEET AND SOUR
SAUCE, SERVED ON
THE SIDE.

• Be careful not to overcook the lotus stem pieces, as they will lose their crunch.

• You can half-fry the fritters in advance, and just before serving, deep-fry to golden brown in hot oil.

LOTUS PEARL KEBABS
Moti Kamal Kebab

INGREDIENTS
¼ cup / 40 g Sago (*saboo dana*)
2 small / 250 g Lotus stems
(*kamal kakdi*), peeled, cut into 1"
slanted pieces (see p. 209)
1 tsp / 5 g Ginger (*adrak*) paste
(see p. 206)
2 tbsp / 12 g Finely-chopped
scallions (*hare pyaz ke patte*)
2 Black cardamom pods (*badi
elaichi*), seeds only, ground
2 tbsp Husked Bengal gram
(*chana atta*), toasted, ground
Salt to taste
Refined vegetable oil for
shallow-frying

To serve:
¾ cup Spicy Tomato Chutney
(*Tikhi Tamatar Chutney*,
see p. 167)

METHOD
- Wash and drain the sago. Place in a sauté pan and pour water exactly up to the level of the sago (adding too much water will make it sticky and spoil the texture); leave covered for 3-4 hours.

- Pressure-cook the lotus stem pieces with 2 cups water to one whistle. Turn off the heat and allow the pressure to drop before removing the lid. (Alternatively, cook in a saucepan until tender.) Drain in a colander and set aside to cool.

- Grate the cooked lotus stem pieces.

- Mix the grated lotus stem with ginger paste, scallions, powdered black cardamom seeds, powdered husked Bengal gram, soaked sago, and salt to taste.

- Divide the mixture into 12-15 equal portions and shape into round, flat patties.

- Pour oil to the depth of ¼" in a flat pan and heat until hot. Add 3-4 patties and, using a slotted spoon, drizzle hot oil from the pan on top of the patties at intervals, until the sides begin to turn light golden brown.

- Flip and fry until evenly light golden brown on the other side; remove and drain on a paper towel. Repeat the process to fry the remaining patties.

- Serve hot accompanied with Spicy Tomato Chutney.

- The toasted and powdered husked Bengal gram can be replaced with gram flour in this recipe.

THIS UNUSUAL LOTUS STEM KEBAB CELEBRATES THE DISTINCTIVE TEXTURE OF SAGO AND THE MILD-SWEETNESS OF BLACK CARDAMOM.

• Sago is a starch extracted from the sago palm. It is also made from tapioca. Shaped like little pearls, sago becomes translucent when cooked.

STUFFED MUSHROOM CAPS
Khumb Ki Katori

INGREDIENTS
25-30 medium Mushrooms
(khumb)
1 tsp / 5 ml Refined
vegetable oil
A few drops Lemon juice
(nimbu ka ras)
2 tsp / 10 ml Light soy sauce
½ tsp / 2½ ml Chili Garlic
Chutney (Lal Lehsuni Chutney,
see p. 166)
1 tbsp / 4 g Finely-chopped
cilantro (dhaniya) leaves
1½ tbsp / 25 ml Balsamic
vinegar

**For the white sauce and pea
mixture:**
2 tsp / 10 ml Refined vegetable
oil
¼ tsp Finely-chopped garlic
(lasan)
¾ tsp All-purpose flour (maida)
1/3 cup / 70 ml (approx) Milk
¼ tsp Sugar
Salt to taste
Freshly-ground black
peppercorns (sabut kali mirch),
to taste
1 tbsp / 15 g Grated cheese
1 cup / 150 g Shelled peas
(hara mattar), cooked
(see p. 210)
2 tbsp / 12 g Finely-chopped
scallions (hare pyaz ke patte)

METHOD
- **For the mushrooms,** carefully remove the stalks and make a slight depression in the center of each mushroom cap (see pic).

- Boil 3¾ cups water; add 1 tsp oil and a few drops of lemon juice. Plunge the mushrooms in the boiling water for 10 seconds; remove and drain in a colander.

- Turn the mushroom caps over and leave to stand for 10 minutes to remove excess water.

- **For the white sauce and pea mixture,** heat 2 tsp oil in a pan for 20 seconds; add the garlic and all-purpose flour and cook on low heat for 20 seconds. Turn off the heat and add the milk, sugar, salt and freshly ground black pepper to taste, and the cheese; mix. Turn the heat back on and bring the white sauce to a boil, stirring constantly.

- Turn off the heat, mix in the cooked peas and scallions; set aside.

- In a bowl, mix the soy sauce and Chili Garlic Chutney. Toss the mushroom caps in the sauce mixture and sprinkle with cilantro leaves.

- **To serve,** arrange the mushroom caps, hollow-side up, on a serving plate and evenly drizzle 1/8 tsp balsamic vinegar inside each cap. Fill the mushroom caps with the white sauce-pea mixture and serve immediately.

- Adding oil and lemon juice to the boiling water gives the mushrooms a luscious sheen and helps preserve their original color.

WITH ITS CHEESY, PEA FILLING AND THE UNEXPECTED HINT OF BALSAMIC VINEGAR, THIS DISH IS AN UNUSUAL TREAT FOR MUSHROOM LOVERS.

• Boil the mushrooms for precisely 10 seconds to ensure that they retain their natural shape and size.

MAIN COURSES

CURRIED GOLDEN DUMPLINGS
Kofte Kacche Kele Ke

INGREDIENTS

For 25 dumplings:

¼ lb / 100 g Paneer (see p. 204)

2 tsp Finely-chopped cilantro (*dhaniya*) leaves

¼ tsp Finely-chopped green chilies

Salt to taste

3 medium / 450 g Green plantains (*kacche kele*, see tip), boiled, peeled, grated (see p. 208)

2 tbsp / 30 g Gram flour (*besan*)

Refined vegetable oil for deep-frying

For the sauce:

3-4 tbsp / 45-60 ml Refined vegetable oil

2 Bay leaves (tej p*atta*)

2 large / 200 g Onions, grated (see p. 213)

1 tsp / 5 g Ginger (*adrak*) paste (see p. 206)

1 tsp / 5 g Green chili paste (see p. 206)

1 tsp / 5 g Turmeric (*haldi*) powder

1 tsp / 5 g Red chili powder

4 large / 400 g Tomatoes, puréed (see p. 213)

Salt to taste

2 tbsp / 30 ml Heavy cream

A pinch Sugar

2 tbsp / 8 g Finely-chopped cilantro (*dhaniya*) leaves, to garnish

For the spice mix, coarsely grind (see p. 213) and set aside:

10 Cashew nuts (*kaju*)

2 Black cardamom pods (*badi elaichi*), seeds only

2 Green cardamom pods (*choti elaichi*), seeds only

½" Cinnamon (*dalchini*) stick

4 Cloves (*laung*)

2 tsp / 10 g Poppyseeds (*khus khus*)

1 tsp / 5 g Cumin (*jeera*) seeds

THIS ROBUSTLY SPICED INDIAN SAUCE MAKES A DELICIOUS COUNTERPOINT TO THE SUBTLE FLAVOR OF THE MODEST GREEN PLANTAINS.

• Plantains are also known as raw, green, or cooking bananas and are available in most supermarkets.

METHOD

- **For the dumplings,** mash the paneer to a smooth paste; mix in the cilantro leaves, green chilies, and salt to taste; set aside.
- Mash the grated plantains to a smooth paste, mix in the gram flour and salt to taste; divide into 25 equal balls.
- Flatten each ball on your palm, place ¼ tsp of the paneer mixture in the center, and shape into round, flat dumplings (*kofte*).
- Pour oil to the depth of 1" in a wok (*kadhai*) and heat until moderately hot. Deep-fry the dumplings in small batches in moderately-hot oil until light golden brown. Remove, drain on a paper towel, and set aside.

- **For the sauce,** heat 3-4 tbsp oil in a pan for 30 seconds; add the bay leaves, grated onions, and ginger and green chili pastes. Fry on low heat until light golden brown, stirring occasionally. Add the turmeric and red chili powders and mix; then add the coarsely-ground spice mixture and mix.
- Add the puréed tomatoes and fry on moderate heat until the oil separates, stirring often to prevent sticking.
- Add 3¾ cups / 750 ml water, salt to taste, and the cream and stir. Gently add the plantains dumplings and a pinch of sugar. Bring the sauce to a boil; then simmer for 8 minutes. Serve hot, garnished with cilantro leaves.

- The fried dumplings can be prepared up to two days in advance and refrigerated. The same can be done for the sauce, up to the stage of adding the puréed tomatoes.

PANEER À LA FENUGREEK
Methi Paneer Pasanda

INGREDIENTS

Refined vegetable oil for cooking
½ lb / 250 g Paneer (see p. 204),
cut into ½" slices
1½ (loosely-packed) cups
Chopped fenugreek leaves
(*methi*)
¼ tsp Sugar (¹/₈ tsp + ¹/₈ tsp)
2 large / 200 g Onions
2 Green cardamom pods (*choti
elaichi*), seeds only, ground (see
p. 219)
½ tsp / 2½ g Turmeric (*haldi*)
powder
¾ tsp / 3¾ g Red chili powder
3 medium / 225 g Tomatoes,
puréed (see p. 213)
2 tbsp / 30 g Yogurt (*dahi*),
slightly sour, whisked
Salt to taste

**For the spice mix, coarsely
grind (see p. 213) and set aside:**
8 Cashew nuts (*kaju*)
2 tsp / 10 g Poppyseeds (*khus
khus*)
2 Green cardamom pods, seeds
only
4 Cloves (*laung*)
½" Cinnamon (*dalchini*) stick

METHOD

• **For the paneer**, heat ¾ tbsp oil in a nonstick pan for
30 seconds; add the paneer slices and sauté on moderate heat
until light brown on both sides (see p. 205). Remove, cut the
slices into 1" cubes, and set aside.

• **For the fenugreek**, heat a pan for 30 seconds; add the fenugreek
leaves and ¹/₈ tsp sugar and cook, covered on moderate heat for
30 seconds. Remove and set aside.

• **For the onions**, peel and cut each onion into eight pieces.
Pressure-cook the onion pieces with 1½ cups / 300 ml water to
one whistle. Simmer for 5 minutes and wait for the pressure to
drop before opening the lid. (Alternatively, cook in a saucepan
until tender.) Cool and coarsely purée in a blender / food
processor; set aside.

• **For the sauce**, heat 2 tbsp oil in a pan for 30 seconds; add the
ground green cardamom seeds and cook on moderate heat for
10 seconds. Add the turmeric and red chili powders and mix.
Add the coarsely-ground spice mix and mix well.

• Add the puréed tomatoes and fry on low heat until the oil
separates, stirring often to prevent sticking. Add the whisked
yogurt and continue frying until the oil separates again.

• Add the cooked fenugreek leaves and fry for 30 seconds.

• Add the sautéed paneer cubes, onion purée, ¹/₈ tsp sugar, and salt
to taste; mix. Bring the sauce to a boil on moderate heat; simmer
for 10 minutes and serve hot.

• Be sure to assemble the spices before preparing the sauce; they are delicate, and
will burn easily if left in the oil longer than required.

THE CASHEW
NUT BASE OF THIS SAUCE
PERFECTLY COMPLEMENTS THE
DISTINCTIVE BITTERNESS OF
FENUGREEK AND THE CAPTIVATING
AROMA OF GREEN
CARDAMOM.

- Whisk the yogurt well before adding it to the sauce, and then stir continuously
  to prevent lumps from forming.

BLACK VELVET LENTILS
Makhmali Dal Makhni

INGREDIENTS

1 cup / 200 g Whole black gram (*sabut urad dal*), soaked in plenty of water for 8 hours or overnight, drained
½ cup / 100 ml Heavy cream
½ cup / 100 g Yogurt (*dahi*), slightly sour, whisked
1 tbsp / 15 g Clarified butter (*ghee*)
1 tsp / 5 g Cumin (*jeera*) seeds
½ tsp / 2½ g Red chili powder
5 large / 500 g Tomatoes, puréed (see p. 213)
Salt to taste
1 tsp / 5 g Sugar
1 tsp / 5 g *Garam masala* powder (see p. 214)
1 tsp / 5 g Butter for serving

For the spice mix:
½ tsp / 2½ g Salt
1" Cinnamon (*dalchini*) stick
2 Bay leaves (tej *patta*)
2 Black cardamom pods (*badi elaichi*)
⅛ tsp Asafoetida (*hing*)
2 tsp / 10 g Finely-chopped ginger (*adrak*)
1 tbsp / 15 ml Mustard oil (*sarson ka tel*) or Clarified butter

For the tempering:
1 tbsp / 15 g Butter
1 tbsp / 15 g Ginger, cut into juliennes
2 Green chilies, slit lengthwise
2 tbsp / 8 g Chopped cilantro (*dhaniya*) leaves
¼ tsp Red chili powder

METHOD

• In a pressure cooker, combine the soaked black gram with the spice mix ingredients and 5 cups / 1 l water. Pressure cook the lentils to one whistle on moderate heat; simmer for 30 minutes and turn off the heat. Once the pressure drops, open the lid. (Alternatively, use 6 cups / 1½ l water and cook in a soup pot until tender.) Cool the lentils and pick out and discard the bay leaves, cinnamon stick, and cardamom pods.

• Lightly mash the lentils with a potato masher or the underside of a ladle. Turn on the heat, bring the mashed lentils to a boil, and cook on moderate heat for 10 minutes. Add the cream and whisked yogurt and simmer for 30 minutes.

• In a separate pan, heat 1 tbsp clarified butter for 30 seconds; add the cumin seeds, red chili powder, and the puréed tomatoes. Cook on high heat for 2 minutes and add to the simmering lentil mixture.

• Bring the mixture to a boil on moderate heat and continue to simmer for 30 minutes. Add salt to taste, sugar, and *garam masala* powder. Continue to simmer for 10 more minutes and transfer to a serving dish.

• **For the tempering,** heat 1 tbsp butter in a tempering ladle for 30 seconds, add the ginger juliennes, and cook for 30 seconds. Now add the slit green chilies, chopped cilantro leaves, and red chili powder; immediately pour over the hot lentils and top with 1 tsp butter; serve hot.

• Unrefined mustard oil brings out the flavor of the black gram.

• The secret to this dish is patience. As described in this recipe, the lentils need to be simmered for a long time to achieve their signature velvety texture.

THIS DISH IS
KNOW AS THE QUEEN OF
DALS AND IS USUALLY
SERVED ON SPECIAL
OCCASIONS.

- For added richness, you may garnish this dish with 1 tbsp heavy cream.

- This lentil dish is best served with Indian breads like Handkerchief Folds (p. 140) or Layered Crispy Bread (p. 142).

CREAMY CURRIED KOFTAS
Kofta Kaju Malai

THE DELICIOUSLY SOFT KOFTAS, STEEPED IN THE CREAMY, SUBTLY-SPICED SAUCE, MAKE THIS DISH THE PERFECT INDULGENCE FOR A SPECIAL OCCASION.

INGREDIENTS
For 20 koftas:
½ lb / 200 g Soft, homemade Paneer (see p. 204),
2 small / 100 g Potatoes, boiled, peeled, grated (see p. 212)
1 tbsp / 4 g Finely-chopped cilantro (*dhaniya*) leaves
1 tsp / 5 g Finely-chopped green chilies
Salt to taste
2 slightly-heaped tbsp / 30 g All-purpose flour (*maida*), for coating
Refined vegetable oil for deep-frying and cooking
2 Bay leaves (*tej patta*)

For the spice mix, coarsely grind (see p. 213) and set aside:
2 Black cardamom pods (*badi elaichi*), seeds only
4 Black peppercorns (*sabut kali mirch*)
4 Cloves (*laung*)
½ tsp / 2½ g Cumin (*jeera*) seeds

For the sauce:
2 tsp / 10 g Poppyseeds (*khus khus*)
2 large / 200 g Onions, grated (see p. 213)
1 tsp / 5 g Ginger (*adrak*) paste (see p. 206)
1 tsp / 5 g Garlic (*lasan*) paste (see p. 206)
1 tsp / 5 g Red chili powder
1 tsp / 5 g Turmeric (*haldi*) powder
2 tbsp / 20 g Cashews (*kaju*), chopped
4 large / 400 g Tomatoes, puréed (see p. 213)
2 tbsp / 30 ml Heavy cream
A pinch Sugar
Salt to taste

To garnish:
2 tbsp / 8 g Finely-chopped cilantro leaves

- For best results, use homemade, rather than packaged, paneer for this recipe.

- It is important to coat the koftas with all-purpose flour and fry them in small batches, so that they do not break.

METHOD

- **For the koftas,** grate the paneer and mash into a fine paste with a rolling pin. Mix with the grated potatoes, cilantro leaves, green chilies, and salt to taste.

- Divide the mixture into 20 equal portions and shape into 2"-long cylinders (koftas). Sprinkle the all-purpose flour on a flat surface and gently roll the koftas on the flour to coat evenly.

- Pour 1" deep oil in a wok (*kadhai*) and heat until moderately hot; deep-fry the koftas in batches of 3-4 on moderate heat until light golden brown. Remove, drain on a paper towel, and set aside.

- **For the sauce,** soak the poppyseeds in ½ cup water for an hour; drain. Using a rolling pin or a traditional Indian stone grinder (*sil-batta*), grind the seeds to a fine paste, adding a little water, if required.

- Heat 3-4 tbsp oil in a pan for 30 seconds; add the bay leaves and the coarsely-ground spice mix.

- Add the grated onion and ginger and garlic pastes and fry on low heat until light golden brown, stirring occasionally. Add the red chili and turmeric powders and mix; add the soaked poppyseed paste and chopped cashew nuts and mix. Add the puréed tomatoes and fry on moderate heat until the oil separates, stirring often to prevent sticking.

- Add ½ cup water, 2 tbsp heavy cream, sugar, and salt to taste. Bring the sauce to a boil and simmer for 5 minutes.

- **To serve,** arrange the koftas in a serving dish and gently pour the hot sauce over them. Garnish with cilantro leaves and serve immediately.

- For added richness, garnish the hot sauce with 2 tbsp heavy cream.
- 8¾ cups / 1¾ l of milk will yield about ½ lb / 200 g of paneer.

CREAMY SAFFRON PANEER
Zafrani Paneer Makhni

INGREDIENTS

Refined vegetable oil
for cooking
½ lb / 250 g Paneer (see p. 204), cut into ½" slices
¼ tsp Saffron (kesar)
1 tsp / 5 ml Screw pine (kewra) water
2 tbsp / 30 g Butter
2 large / 200 g Onions, grated (see p. 213)
1 tsp / 5 g Ginger (adrak) paste (see p. 206)
1 tsp / 5 g Garlic (lasan) paste (see p. 206)
½ tsp / 2½ g Red chili powder
1½ cups / 300 g Yogurt (dahi), slightly sour, whisked
4 Green chilies, slit lengthwise
A pinch Sugar
Salt to taste

For the spice mix, coarsely grind (see p. 213) and set aside:
2 tsp / 10 g Poppyseeds (khus khus)
10 Cashew nuts (kaju)
2 tbsp / 20 g Peanuts (moongphalli), skinned (see p. 215)
4 Green cardamom pods (choti elaichi), seeds only
4 Cloves (laung)
½" Cinnamon (dalchini) stick

METHOD

• Heat 1 tbsp oil in a pan for 30 seconds; sauté the paneer slices on moderate heat until light golden brown on both sides (see p. 205). Remove, cut into 1" cubes, and set aside.

• In a mortar, soak the saffron in the screw pine water for 5 minutes; grind to a smooth paste with a mortar and pestle and set aside.

• Heat 2 tbsp butter and 1 tbsp oil in a wok (kadhai) for 30 seconds; add the grated onions and ginger and garlic pastes and fry on low heat until light golden brown, stirring occasionally.

• Add the red chili powder and the coarsely-ground spice mix and mix well.

• Add the whisked yogurt and cook until the oil separates, stirring frequently.

• Add the sautéed paneer cubes, ¾-1 cup / 175-200 ml water, saffron and screw pine water paste, slit green chilies, a pinch of sugar, and salt to taste; mix gently. Bring the sauce to a boil on moderate heat, simmer for 5 minutes and serve hot.

THE EXOTIC INDIAN FLAVORS OF SAFFRON AND SCREW PINE WATER AND THE NUTTY OVERTONE OF CASHEW NUTS GIVE THIS RICH PANEER RECIPE A ROYAL TOUCH.

• Adding oil along with the butter ensures that the butter clarifies without burning, keeping the flavor intact.

• Screw pine water is a fragrant, sweet essence distilled from the screw pine (*kewra*) or *Pandanus fascicularis* flower. It is used to flavor sweet and savory Indian dishes.

ᴅIAN CHEESE FLORENTINE
Paneer Bahaar

INGREDIENTS

1½ lb / 750 g Spinach (*palak*)
½ tsp / 2½ g Sugar
2-3 tbsp / 30-45 ml Refined vegetable oil
2 medium / 150 g Onions, grated (see p. 213)
1 tsp / 5 g Ginger (*adrak*) paste (see p. 206)
¼ tsp Garlic (*lasan*) paste (see p. 206)
¾ tsp / 3¾ g Red chili powder
½ lb / 250 g Paneer (see p. 204), cut into 1" cubes
Salt to taste

For the spice mix, coarsely grind (see p. 213) and set aside:

2 Black cardamom pods (*badi elaichi*), seeds only
4 Cloves (*laung*)
½" Cinnamon (*dalchini*) stick
8 Black peppercorns (*sabut kali mirch*)

To serve:

1 tbsp / 15 ml Heavy cream
1 tbsp / 15 g Butter

METHOD

- **For the spinach,** cut off and discard the hard stems, chop the tender leaves, and wash in a colander.

- Heat a pan for 30 seconds and add the chopped spinach and sugar. Cook, covered, on moderate heat for 2 minutes. Remove from the pan and cool.

- Finely chop the spinach in food processor along with any residual water and set aside.

- **For the sauce,** heat 2-3 tbsp oil in a pan for 30 seconds; add the grated onions and ginger and garlic pastes and fry on low heat until light golden brown, stirring occasionally.

- Add the red chili powder and the ground spice mix and mix well.

- Add the paneer cubes, spinach, and salt to taste; mix gently. Bring the sauce to a boil on moderate heat, simmer for 5 minutes, and transfer to a serving dish.

- **To serve,** heat a pan for 20 seconds, add the cream and mix with a spatula for 5 seconds over moderate heat; pour over the sauce. Repeat the process with the butter and serve immediately.

THIS DELICIOUS NORTH INDIAN DISH REVELS IN THE NATURAL, EARTHY FLAVOR OF SPINACH, HIGHLIGHTED BY FRESHLY-GROUND SPICES AND A SUBTLE HINT OF GARLIC.

- This spinach sauce base can be paired with par-cooked mushrooms, corn, or a vegetable medley instead of paneer.

- For the sauce to retain its fresh green color, add the spinach and follow the subsequent steps just before serving.

 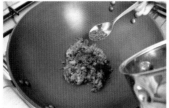  

• This dish can be served with Fenugreek Maize Bread (see p. 144).

SPICY GOLDEN FLORETS
Sunhere Rangeele Phool

INGREDIENTS

2 medium / 1 kg Cauliflowers (*phool gobi*), cut into 20-25 florets, about 1½" in size
Refined vegetable oil for cooking and deep-frying
2 medium / 150 g Onions, grated (see p. 213)
1 tsp / 5 g Ginger (*adrak*) paste (see p. 206)
1 tsp / 5 g Garlic (*lasan*) paste (see p. 206)
1 tsp / 5 g Red chili powder
1 tsp / 5 g Turmeric (*haldi*) powder
4 large / 400 g Tomatoes, puréed (see p. 213)
2 tbsp / 30 g Green peas (*hara mattar*), cooked (see p. 210)
Salt to taste
1 tsp / 5 g *Garam masala* powder (see p. 214)
2 tbsp / 8 g Finely-chopped cilantro (*dhaniya*) leaves

METHOD

- Bring 5 cups water to a boil with ½ tsp salt; add the florets and cook on high heat for a minute. Drain in a colander and dry on a paper towel.

- Pour oil to the depth of 1" in a wok (*kadhai*) and heat until moderately hot. Deep-fry the florets in batches until light golden brown.

- Remove, drain on a paper towel, and set aside.

- Heat 2-3 tbsp oil in a pan for 30 seconds; add the grated onions and ginger and garlic pastes and fry on low heat until light golden brown, stirring occasionally. Add the red chili and turmeric powders and mix.

- Add the puréed tomatoes and fry on moderate heat until the oil separates, stirring often to prevent sticking.

- Add the fried florets, cooked peas, and salt to taste; mix gently and cook on low heat for 2 minutes.

- Add the *garam masala* powder and cilantro leaves, mix, and serve hot.

- If raw cauliflower florets are deep-fried, they become leathery. Par-boiling them for a minute ensures a firm, yet tender texture.

THIS SIMPLE RECIPE SHOWCASES THE POPULAR INDIAN ONION-TOMATO COMBINATION, USED AS A SAUCE BASE FOR MANY DELICIOUS DISHES.

HERB 'N' SPICE POTATOES
Dum Aloo Chaman

THE UNUSUAL COMBINATION OF FENUGREEK AND WHOLE MILK FUDGE CREATES A UNIQUE BITTER-SWEET INDIAN SAUCE.

INGREDIENTS
20 / 500 g Small potatoes, about 2" in size
1 (tightly-packed) cup Chopped fenugreek (*methi*) leaves
¼ tsp Sugar (¹/₈ tsp + ¹/₈ tsp)
Salt to taste
Refined vegetable oil for cooking and deep-frying

For the sauce:
2 medium / 150 g Onions, grated (see p. 213)
½ tsp / 2½ g Ginger (*adrak*) paste (see p. 206)
½ tsp / 2½ g Green chili paste (see p. 206)
½ tsp / 2½ g Red chili powder
½ tsp / 2½ g Turmeric (*haldi*) powder
3 medium / 225 g Tomatoes, puréed (see p. 213)
¼ cup / 50 g Yogurt (*dahi*), slightly sour, whisked
2 oz / 50 g Whole milk fudge (*khoya*), grated (see p. 203)

For the spice mix, coarsely grind (see p. 213) and set aside:
½ tsp / 2½ g Cumin (*jeera*) seeds
2 Cloves (*laung*)
1 Black cardamom (*badi elaichi*), seeds only
4 Black peppercorns (*sabut kali mirch*)
¼" Cinnamon (*dalchini*) stick

METHOD
- Peel and cut each potato in half, breadthwise; prick each piece gently with a fork and immerse in water. Remove and pat dry with a paper towel when ready to use.

- Heat a pan for 30 seconds; add the chopped fenugreek and ¹/₈ tsp sugar. Cook, covered, on moderate heat for 30 seconds; remove and set aside.

- Pour oil to the depth of 1" in a wok (*kadhai*) and heat until moderately hot. Deep-fry the potato pieces in moderately-hot oil until light golden brown, turning occasionally. Remove, drain on a paper towel, and set aside.

- **For the sauce**, heat 3-4 tbsp oil in a pan for 30 seconds; add the grated onions and ginger and chili pastes and fry on low heat until light golden brown, stirring occasionally. Add the red chili and turmeric powders and mix; add the coarsely-ground spice mix and mix well.

- Add the puréed tomatoes and fry on moderate heat until the oil separates, stirring often to prevent sticking.

- Add the whisked yogurt and fry on low heat until the oil separates again, stirring frequently.

- Add the grated whole milk fudge and cook for a minute.

- Add the fenugreek leaves and cook for 30 seconds.

- Add the deep-fried potatoes pieces, 1¼ cups / 250 ml water, ¹/₈ tsp sugar, and salt to taste. Bring the sauce to a boil on moderate heat, simmer for 10 minutes and serve hot.

- The potato pieces can be deep-fried and the fenugreek leaves cooked up to two days in advance and refrigerated.

- This sauce can be used for a variety of ingredients including paneer, mushrooms, corn, or vegetable dumplings (koftas).

SMOKEY PEPPERS 'N' PANEER
Paneer Bhari Shimla Mirch

INGREDIENTS

4 / 150 g Small onions, about
1¼" in size
1 tbsp / 15 g Butter
2 tbsp / 30 ml Refined
vegetable oil
1 tsp / 5 g Ginger (adrak) paste
(see p. 206)
1 tsp / 5 g Green chili paste
(see p. 206)
½ tsp / 2½ g Red chili powder
1½ cups / 300 g Yogurt (dahi),
slightly sour, whisked
½ lb / 250 g Masala paneer (see
p. 205), cut into ½" cubes
2 tbsp / 30 ml Heavy cream,
lightly whisked
½ cup / 100 ml Milk
¼ tsp Sugar
Salt to taste
3 medium / 300 g Yellow bell
peppers, deseeded and halved
lengthwise
3 medium / 300 g Red bell
peppers, deseeded and halved
lengthwise

**For the spice mix, coarsely
grind (see p. 213) and set aside:**
1½ tsp / 7½ g Poppyseeds
(khus khus)
1 tsp / 5 g Cumin (jeera) seeds
4 Green cardamom pods (choti
elaichi), seeds only
4 Cloves (laung)
½" Cinnamon (dalchini) stick
8 Almonds (badam), soaked
in hot water for 10 minutes,
peeled, and dried on a
paper towel

METHOD

• **For the onions,** prick each onion all over with a fork, pierce
  with a skewer or fork, and roast directly over an open flame,
  until charred on top and soft inside (this usually takes about
  15 minutes).

• Peel off the charred layer and wash and grind the soft portion to
  a smooth paste in a blender / food processor; set aside.

• **For the sauce,** heat 1 tbsp butter along with 1 tbsp oil in a pan
  for 30 seconds; add the onion paste and ginger and green chili
  pastes and fry on low heat until light brown, stirring occasionally.

• Add the red chili powder and the coarsely-ground spice mix and
  mix well.

• Add the whisked yogurt and fry on low heat until the oil
  separates, stirring frequently. Add the masala paneer cubes,
  whisked heavy cream, milk, sugar and salt to taste; mix gently.
  Bring the sauce to a boil on moderate heat and simmer for 5
  minutes.

• To check if the onions have roasted adequately, press them between
  your thumb and forefinger; they should feel soft.

• Heat 1 tbsp oil in a pan for 30 seconds; add the yellow and red bell pepper halves and cook on high heat for 30 seconds, tossing frequently. Sprinkle with salt to taste and arrange on a serving dish hollow-side up. Gently spoon the hot paneer sauce into the sautéed bell pepper halves and serve immediately.

THE SMOKINESS OF THE ROASTED ONIONS, THE SUBTLE SPICE OF THE PANEER, AND THE CRUNCH OF THE PEPPERS CREATE A DELECTABLE SYMPHONY OF FLAVORS AND TEXTURES.

• This flavorful and rich sauce can be used as a base to make other variations with your favorite sautéed vegetables.

SPINACH DUMPLINGS IN YOGURT SAUCE
Palak Kofta Kadhi

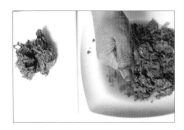   

INGREDIENTS

For 20-25 dumplings:
1½ lb / 750 g Spinach (*palak*)
2 medium / 150 g Potatoes, boiled, peeled, grated (see p. 208)
3 tbsp / 45 g Gram flour (*besan*)
Salt to taste

For the sauce (*kadhi*):
2 cups / 400 g Sour yogurt (*dahi*)
2 tbsp / 30 g Gram flour (*besan*)
2 tsp / 10 g Ginger (*adrak*) paste (see p. 206)
1 tsp / 5 g Green chili paste (see p. 206)
¼ tsp Sugar
¼ tsp Turmeric (*haldi*) powder
Salt to taste
2 tbsp / 8 g Finely-chopped cilantro (*dhaniya*) leaves

For the tempering:
1 tbsp / 15 g Clarified butter (*ghee*)
⅛ tsp Asafoetida (*hing*)
½ tsp / 2½ g Cumin (*jeera*) seeds
½ tsp / 2½ g Red chili powder
2 Dried red chilies (*sookhi lal mirch*), broken

THIS LOW CALORIE ENTRÉE OF NUTRITIOUS SPINACH DUMPLINGS IN SPICY YOGURT SAUCE TASTES BEST WITH STEAMED RICE OR ANY INDIAN WHEAT BREAD.

METHOD

- **For the dumplings (*kofta*),** cut off and discard the hard stems of the spinach, and finely chop the leaves. Wash the chopped spinach and dry on a paper towel. Place in a microwave-safe bowl and microwave on high for 2 minutes. Alternately, heat a pan for 30 seconds, add the spinach, and cook, covered, on high heat for a 1½ minutes. Cool the spinach and squeeze out any water. Mash using the underside of a spoon.

- Mix the mashed spinach with the grated potatoes, gram flour, and salt to taste.

- Divide the mixture into 20-25 equal portions and shape into round dumplings.

- Arrange the dumplings in a greased baking dish, making sure that they don't touch each other. Brush them all over with oil. Preheat the oven at 200°C / 400°F for 10 minutes and bake the dumplings for 15 minutes; remove and set aside.

- **For the sauce (*kadhi*),** whisk together the yogurt and gram flour to a smooth paste. Add the ginger and green chili pastes, sugar, turmeric powder, salt to taste, and 2 cups / 475 ml water; mix.

- Transfer to a deep pan and bring the sauce to a boil on moderate heat, stirring frequently. Simmer for 10 minutes and set aside.

- Add the spinach dumplings to the sauce, turn the heat back on, and bring the mixture to a boil. Add the cilantro leaves, mix, and transfer to a serving dish.

- **For the tempering,** heat 1 tbsp clarified butter in a pan for 10 seconds; add the asafoetida, cumin seeds, red chili powder, and broken red chilies; immediately pour over the sauce and serve hot.

- Add the spinach dumplings and the chopped cilantro leaves to the yogurt sauce just before serving. This ensures that the dumplings don't become soggy and the cilantro retains its fresh flavor.

  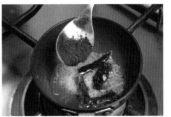 

- As an alternative, you can steam the dumplings for 15 minutes or fry them with a little oil in a special South Indian pan called a *kuzhi* *paniyaram* or a pancake puff pan (see last step pic).

LENTIL DUMPLINGS IN SPICY SAUCE
Taazi Mangodi Ki Sabzi

INGREDIENTS

¾ cup / 125 g Skinned, split green gram lentils (*dhuli moong dal*), soaked in plenty of water for 3 hours, drained

Refined vegetable oil for deep-frying

1-2 tbsp / 15-30 g Clarified butter (*ghee*)

A pinch Asafoetida (*hing*)

½ tsp / 2½ g Cumin (*jeera*) seeds

1 tsp / 5 g Ginger (*adrak*) paste (see p. 206)

½ tsp / 2½ g Green chili paste (see p. 206)

¼ tsp Turmeric (*haldi*) powder

½ tsp / 2½ g Red chili powder

3 medium / 225 g Tomatoes, puréed (see p. 213)

1 cup / 200 g Yogurt (*dahi*), slightly sour, whisked

Salt to taste

2 tbsp / 8 g Finely-chopped cilantro (*dhaniya*) leaves to garnish

METHOD

- **For the dumplings (*mangodi*),** grind the soaked green gram to a thick batter in a blender / food processor, using very little water. Transfer the batter to a large bowl and, using a hand beater, whisk until light and fluffy. Test by dropping ¼ tsp of the batter in ½ cup water. If the batter floats, it is of the right consistency for soft dumplings. Reserve 2 tsp of the batter for use in the sauce.

- Pour oil to the depth of 1" in a wok (*kadhai*) and heat until near-smoking point. Drop in small portions of the batter with your fingers, a few at a time, and deep-fry in hot oil until evenly light golden brown.

- Remove the dumplings with a slotted spoon and immediately immerse in 4¼ cups / 1 l of salted water (see tip) for an hour.

- Remove; squeeze gently between your palms to remove the excess water and set aside.

- **For the sauce,** mix 2 tsp of the reserved batter with 3½ cups / 825 ml water; set aside. Heat the clarified butter in a pan for 30 seconds; add the asafoetida, cumin seeds, ginger and green chili pastes, and turmeric and red chili powders; mix.

- Add the puréed tomatoes and fry on moderate heat until the oil separates, stirring often to prevent sticking.

- Add the whisked yogurt and fry on low heat, stirring continuously until the mixture comes to a boil. Continue frying until the oil separates again, stirring occasionally.

- Add the watered-batter mixture to the sauce and bring to a boil on moderate heat, stirring occasionally.

- Add the squeezed dumplings and salt to taste and bring to a boil again. Simmer for 10 minutes, sprinkle on cilantro leaves, and serve hot.

- To make salted water, mix 1 tsp of salt with 5 cups of water at room temperature.

- The reserved batter acts as a binder when added to the sauce, giving it body and a smooth consistency.

AN
INTRINSIC PART
OF A FORMAL MEAL IN
THE NORTHERN STATE OF
UTTAR PRADESH, THIS MILDLY
SPICED DISH IS BEST SERVED
WITH INDIAN WHEAT
BREADS.

• Immersing the dumplings in salted water immediately after deep-frying removes excess oil and gives the dumplings a soft texture.

LENTIL NUGGET CURRY
Chattpatte Gatte

INGREDIENTS

For the nuggets (*gatte*):
2 cups / 200 g Gram flour (*besan*)
1 tsp / 5 g Fennel (*saunf*) seeds
1 tsp / 5 g Cumin (*jeera*) seeds
1 tsp / 5 g Red chili powder
½ tsp / 2½ g Turmeric (*haldi*) powder
1 tsp / 5 g Coriander (*dhaniya*) seeds
1 tsp / 5 g *Garam masala* powder (see p. 214)
1 tsp / 5 g Mint (*pudina*) powder
1 tsp / 5 g Salt
4 tbsp / 60 ml Refined vegetable oil

For the sauce:
1½ cups / 300 g Yogurt (*dahi*), slightly sour
½ tsp / 2½ g Gram flour
Salt to taste
2 tbsp / 8 g Finely-chopped cilantro (*dhaniya*) leaves
1 tsp / 5 g *Garam masala* powder (see p. 214)
1 tsp / 5 g Mint powder

For the tempering:
2½ tbsp / 40 g Clarified butter (*ghee*) or Refined vegetable oil
¼ tsp Asafoetida (*hing*)
2 tsp / 10 g Cumin seeds
1 tsp / 5 g Fennel seeds
2 tsp / 10 g Finely-chopped ginger (*adrak*)
1 tsp / 5 g Finely-chopped green chilies
1 tsp / 5 g Turmeric powder
1 tsp / 5 g Red chili powder
3 tsp / 15 g Coriander powder

METHOD

- **For the nuggets (*gatte*),** sift the gram flour and mix in the fennel and cumin seeds, red chili and turmeric powders, coriander seeds, *garam masala*, mint powder, salt, and oil.

- Knead into a semi-hard dough, adding water until you achieve the desired texture. Divide the dough into 8 equal portions and shape into ½"-thick cylinders.

- In a large pot, boil 5 cups water, gently lower the cylinders into the water, and cook on high heat until they float to the surface.

- Drain in a colander, reserving the stock for use later in the sauce.

- Cool the cylinders and cut into ¼" nuggets.

- Ensure the reserved stock is at room temperature before whisking with the yogurt, as using hot stock will cause the yogurt to separate.

- The nuggets (*gatte*) and the stock can be made up to a day in advance and stored separately in the refrigerator.

- **For the sauce,** whisk the yogurt with ½ tsp gram flour and the reserved stock (at room temperature) until smooth; set aside.

- **For the tempering,** heat 2½ tbsp clarified butter in a pan for 30 seconds; add the asafoetida, cumin and fennel seeds, finely chopped ginger and green chilies, turmeric, red chili, and coriander powders and mix.

- Add the whisked yogurt mixture and bring to a boil on moderate heat, stirring continuously.

- Add the nuggets and salt to taste; bring the sauce to a boil again; simmer for 8 minutes.

- Add the cilantro leaves, *garam masala*, and mint powder and mix gently. Simmer for 2 minutes and serve hot.

THIS TRADITIONAL AND WHOLESOME DISH FROM THE NORTHWESTERN STATE OF RAJASTHAN CAN BE SERVED WITH STEAMED RICE OR PLAIN INDIAN BREAD.

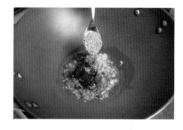

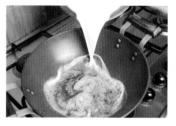

- The nuggets can also be deep-fried and served as an appetizer, along with Sweet 'n' Sour Chutney (p. 165) or Green Coconut Chutney (p. 171).

NUTTY GREEN BEANS
Tilwali Phalli

INGREDIENTS

½ lb / 250 g Green beans
½ tsp / 2½ g Sugar
2 tsp / 10 g White sesame seeds
(*safed til*)
1 tbsp / 15 ml Refined
vegetable oil
1 tsp / 5 g Chopped garlic (*lasan*)
1 tbsp / 4 g Finely-chopped
Parsley or cilantro (*dhaniya*)
leaves
Salt to taste
Black peppercorns (*sabut kali
mirch*), freshly ground, to taste

To garnish:
2 tbsp / 30 ml Refined
vegetable oil
2 tbsp / 20 g Peanuts
(*moongphalli*), skinned
(see p. 215)

METHOD

- String the green beans, if necessary, and cut them into 3-4" slanted pieces. Boil 3¾ cups water; add ½ tsp sugar and the beans. Blanch for 5-6 minutes until the beans are tender; strain in a colander and wash under cold running water (see tip).

- Heat a pan for 30 seconds; add the sesame seeds and dry-toast on low heat, stirring constantly, until evenly light golden brown; remove and set aside.

- Heat 1 tbsp oil in a pan for 30 seconds; add the garlic and blanched beans. Sauté on high heat for 1-2 minutes. Add the parsley or cilantro leaves, sesame seeds, and salt and pepper to taste; toss for 30 seconds. Transfer to a serving dish.

- **To garnish,** heat 2 tbsp oil in a pan for 30 seconds; add the skinned peanuts and fry on low heat until light golden brown, stirring constantly. Sprinkle over the beans and serve hot.

> THE DELICATE FLAVOR OF THE GREEN BEANS IS HIGHLIGHTED BY THE SMOKY, NUTTY CRUNCH OF SESAME AND PEANUT.

- Blanching is a process in which vegetables are added to boiling water for a brief, timed period and then plunged into cold water, or held under running water to stop them from cooking further. This process is used to retain both the texture of the vegetables as well as their fresh, natural color.

SPICY GREEN JACKFRUIT
Sukkha Kathal

INGREDIENTS

2¼ lbs / 1 kg Unripened jackfruit (*kathal*)
1½ tsp / 7½ g Red chili powder
3 tsp / 15 g Coriander (*dhaniya*) powder
1 tsp / 5 g Dried mango (*amchur*) powder
Salt to taste
2 tbsp / 8 g Finely-chopped cilantro (*dhaniya*) leaves, to garnish

For the seasoning:

3-4 tbsp / 45-60 ml Unrefined mustard oil (*sarson ka tel*)
¼ tsp Asafoetida (*hing*)
½ tsp / 2½ g Carom (*ajwain*) seeds
¼ tsp Turmeric (*haldi*) powder
1½ tbsp / 25 g Gram flour (*besan*)

METHOD

• Apply vegetable oil generously to your palms and knife and peel the jackfruit, discarding the outer skin. Cut the remaining vegetable into 1½" pieces. Pressure-cook the pieces with 4 cups water to one whistle. Wait until the pressure drops and remove the lid. (Alternatively, cook in soup pot until tender.) Drain in a colander and set aside to cool (see p. 209). Remove the seeds and discard their hard cover.

• Press the jackfruit flesh and seeds between your palms to remove any excess water.

• Heat 3-4 tbsp mustard oil in a pan for 30 seconds; add the asafoetida, carom seeds, turmeric powder, and gram flour, and cook on moderate heat for 10 seconds. Add the jackfruit pieces along with the seeds and mix.

• Add the red chili, coriander, and dried mango powders and salt to taste; mix. Cook on low heat until the jackfruit turns a golden brown color, stirring occasionally (this will take about 30-40 minutes). Add the cilantro leaves, mix, and serve hot.

• Removing the outer skin of the jackfruit can be a time-consuming process. You may be able to find it ready-skinned.

• If mustard oil is not available, you can substitute any vegetable oil.
• This dish can be stored for up to a week in the refrigerator.

TROPICAL JACKFRUIT CURRY
Rasedaar Kathal

INGREDIENTS

Refined vegetable oil for
cooking and deep-frying
3 cups / 300 g Tender, skinned
unripened jackfruit (kathal), cut
into 1" cubes (see p. 209)
1½ cups / 300 g Yogurt (dahi),
slightly sour
½ tsp / 2½ g Gram flour (besan)
2 medium / 150 g Onions,
grated (see p. 213)
2 tsp / 10 g Ginger (adrak)
paste (see p. 206)
1 tsp / 5 g Green chili paste
(see p. 206)
½ tsp / 2½ g Turmeric (haldi)
powder
¾ tsp / 3¾ g Red chili powder
3 medium / 225 g Tomatoes,
puréed (see p. 213)
Salt to taste
2 tbsp / 8 g Finely-chopped
cilantro (dhaniya) leaves
½ tsp / 2½ g Garam masala
powder (see p. 214)

METHOD

- Pour oil to the depth of 1" in a wok (kadhai) and heat until
  moderately hot. In batches, deep-fry the jackfruit pieces until light
  golden brown. Remove, drain on paper towel, and set aside.

- Whisk the yogurt with gram flour until smooth and set aside.

- Heat 2-3 tbsp oil in a pan for 30 seconds; add the grated onions,
  ginger paste, and green chili paste and cook on low heat until light
  golden brown, stirring occasionally.

- Add the turmeric and red chili powders and mix. Add the puréed
  tomatoes and fry on moderate heat until the oil separates,
  stirring often to prevent sticking.

- Add the yogurt-gram flour mixture and cook on low heat until
  the oil separates again, stirring frequently.

- Add the fried jackfruit pieces, 1¾ cups / 400 ml water, and salt to
  taste. Bring the sauce to a boil on moderate heat and simmer for
  8 minutes. Sprinkle the cilantro leaves and garam masala powder
  over the sauce; serve hot.

THIS RICHLY-SPICED SAUCE
PERFECTLY BALANCES THE
UNRIPENED JACKFRUIT, WHICH
HAS A SUBTLE FLAVOR AND
FLESHY TEXTURE.

- For deep-frying, always pick tender, unripened jackfruit with small seeds. The older
  fruits tend to have a harder skin that is inedible and tough to remove after frying.

- This dish is best accompanied by steamed rice or freshly-made plain, Indian breads like *phulkas* or *parathas*.

ZESTY ZUCCHINI LENTILS
Anokhi Moong Dal

INGREDIENTS

2½ tsp / 12½ g Clarified butter (*ghee*) (½ tsp + 2 tsp)

1 cup / 200 g Skinned, split green gram (*dhuli moong dal*), washed, soaked in plenty of water for 15 minutes, drained

½ tsp / 2½ g Turmeric (*haldi*) powder

Salt to taste

1 small / 100 g Zucchini, cut into 1" slanted pieces

½ cup / 60 g Cherry tomatoes

2 tbsp / 8 g Finely-chopped cilantro (*dhaniya*) leaves

For the tempering:

1 tbsp / 15 g Clarified butter

2 tsp / 10 g Ginger (*adrak*), cut into juliennes

A pinch Asafoetida (*hing*)

½ tsp / 2½ g Cumin (*jeera*) seeds

2 Cloves (*laung*)

2 Green cardamom pods (*choti elaichi*)

¼ tsp Freshly-ground black peppercorns (*sabut kali mirch*)

METHOD

• Heat a pressure cooker for 30 seconds; add ½ tsp clarified butter, soaked green gram, 2 cups / 500 ml water, turmeric powder, and salt to taste, pressure-cook to one whistle. Turn off the heat, let the pressure drop, and remove the lid. (Alternatively, use 2½ cups / 600 ml water and cook in a soup pot until tender.)

• Heat 2 tsp clarified butter in a pan for 30 seconds; add the zucchini pieces and cherry tomatoes. Sauté on moderate heat for a minute, stirring frequently. Remove and add to the cooked lentils.

• Bring the lentils to a boil on high heat. Add the cilantro leaves, mix well, and transfer to a serving dish.

• **For the tempering,** heat 1 tbsp clarified butter in a tempering ladle for 30 seconds; add the ginger juliennes and cook on moderate heat for a minute, stirring occasionally. Add the asafoetida, cumin seeds, cloves, green cardamom pods, and black pepper; pour over the lentils immediately and serve hot.

THE COMBINATION OF ZUCCHINI AND CHERRY TOMATOES GIVES THIS ATTRACTIVE DISH A DELICIOUS TWIST

• Skinned, split green gram tends to cook quickly. To avoid overcooking, monitor the soaking and cooking time carefully.

SPICED LEAFY LENTILS
Chatpata Chana Palak

INGREDIENTS
2 (loosely-packed) cups Spinach (*palak*), chopped, washed in a colander
¼ tsp Sugar
¾ cup / 125 g Husked, split Bengal gram (*chana dal*), washed, soaked in plenty of water for 1 hour, drained
½ tsp / 2½ g Turmeric (*haldi*) powder
2 Black cardamom pods (*badi elaichi*)
1½" Cinnamon (*dalchini*) stick
Salt to taste
2 tsp / 10 g Chopped ginger (*adrak*)
½ tsp / 2½ g Chopped green chilies
1 medium / 75 g Tomato, grated (see p. 212)
1 large / 100 g Tomato, roasted, peeled, cut into cubes (see p. 212)

For the tempering:
1½ tbsp / 25 g Clarified butter (*ghee*)
1 medium / 75 g Onion, cut into long slices
½ tsp / 2½ g Cumin (*jeera*) seeds
4 Dried red chilies (*sookhi lal mirch*)
½ tsp / 2½ g Red chili powder

METHOD
• Heat a pan for 30 seconds; add the spinach and ¼ tsp sugar and cook, covered, on moderate heat for a minute. Remove and cool. Lightly mash the cooked spinach using the underside of a spoon.

• Pressure-cook the Bengal gram with 2 cups / 500 ml water, turmeric, black cardamom pods, cinnamon stick, and salt to taste to one whistle. Simmer for 12 minutes and turn off the heat. Wait until the pressure drops and remove the lid. (Alternatively, use 2½ cups / 600 ml water and cook in a soup pot until tender.) Add the ginger, green chilies, grated tomato, and roasted tomato cubes. Bring the mixture to a boil on moderate heat. Add the mashed spinach and bring to a boil again; simmer for 2 minutes and transfer to a serving dish.

• **For the tempering,** heat 1½ tbsp clarified butter in a tempering ladle for 30 seconds; add the onion slices and fry on moderate heat until light brown, stirring frequently. Add the cumin seeds, dried red chilies, and red chili powder; immediately pour over the lentils and serve hot.

> THIS IS A HEALTHY LENTIL CURRY THAT DRAWS ITS SUBTLE FLAVORS FROM TWO CELEBRATED INDIAN SPICES: CINNAMON AND CARDAMOM.

• Soaking the lentils for an hour ahead of time ensures that they cook quickly.

• Add the mashed spinach to the lentils just before serving so that the spinach retains its natural green color.

CLASSIC CURRY TRIO
Tiranga Aloo Ta-Mattar

INGREDIENTS

1-2 tbsp / 15-30 ml Refined vegetable oil

A pinch Asafoetida (*hing*)

½ tsp / 2½ g Cumin (*jeera*) seeds

2 tsp / 10 g Chopped ginger (*adrak*)

½ tsp / 2½ g Chopped green chilies

¼ tsp Turmeric (*haldi*) powder

⅓ tsp Red chili powder

3 medium / 225 g Tomatoes, puréed (see p. 213)

1 cup / 150 g Green peas (*hara mattar*), cooked (see p. 210)

2 medium / 150 g Potatoes, boiled (see p. 208), peeled, cut into 1" cubes

Salt to taste

¼ tsp *Garam masala* powder (see p. 214)

2 tbsp / 8 g Finely-chopped cilantro (*dhaniya*) leaves

METHOD

- Heat 1-2 tbsp oil in a pan for 30 seconds; add the asafoetida, cumin seeds, ginger, green chilies, turmeric, and red chili powder; mix.

- Add the puréed tomatoes and fry on moderate heat until the oil separates, stirring often to prevent sticking. Add the cooked peas and cook on high heat for 30 seconds, stirring continuously.

- Add the potato cubes, 1 cup / 250 ml water, and salt to taste; bring the sauce to a boil; then simmer for 5 minutes. Add the *garam masala* powder and cilantro leaves; mix and serve immediately.

THIS SPICY COMBINATION OF POTATOES, PEAS, AND TOMATOES IS AN ALL-TIME FAVORITE, ENJOYED YEAR-ROUND IN NORTH INDIA.

- When available, use fresh, tender peas for this recipe. However, frozen peas may also be used.

- During winter, this dish is enjoyed with seasonal specialty breads like Stuffed Millet Bread (p. 148) and Masala Maize Puffs (p. 150).

GARDEN GREEN PEAS
Hare Bhare Mattar

DELICATELY SPICED WITH GINGER, THIS VERSATILE DISH CAN BE EATEN FOR BREAKFAST, LUNCH, OR DINNER. AT BREAKFAST, IT GOES BY THE QUAINT NAME OF GHUGNI AND IS OFTEN EATEN WITH GOLDEN-BROWN TOAST.

INGREDIENTS
1 tbsp / 15 ml Refined vegetable oil
A pinch Asafoetida (*hing*)
½ tsp / 2½ g Cumin (*jeera*) seeds
½ oz / 10 g Ginger (*adrak*), cut into 1" juliennes (2 tsp)
1 Green chili, slit
2 cups / 300 g Green peas (*hara mattar*)
¼ tsp Sugar
Salt to taste
¼ tsp *Garam masala* powder (see p. 214)
2 tbsp / 8 g Finely-chopped cilantro (*dhaniya*) leaves

METHOD
• Heat 1 tbsp oil in a wok (*kadhai*) for 30 seconds; add the asafoetida, cumin seeds, ginger, and green chili and sauté on moderate heat for 10 seconds.

• Add the peas, sugar, and salt to taste; mix well. Cover and cook on low heat, stirring occasionally until the peas are tender, but still firm. If you find any residual water, uncover and cook on high heat until it evaporates.

• Add the *garam masala* powder and cilantro leaves; mix and serve immediately.

• The signature element of this dish is its natural aroma and flavor. That is why it is best to use freshly shelled (and not frozen) peas.

• After transferring to a serving dish, keep covered with a wire mesh, rather than a lid, so that the peas retain their fresh, green color.

MINTY MUSHROOM MEDLEY
Khumb Mattar Mela

INGREDIENTS

Refined vegetable oil for
cooking
2-3 drops Lemon juice (*nimbu
ka ras*)
25 medium / 250 g Mushrooms
(*khumb*), halved
2 medium / 150 g Onions,
grated (see p. 213)
½ tsp / 2½ g Ginger (*adrak*)
paste (see p. 206)
½ tsp / 2½ g Garlic (*lasan*)
paste (see p. 206)
¼ tsp Red chili powder
¾ cup / 150 g Yogurt (*dahi*),
slightly sour, whisked
2 cups / 300 g Green peas
(*hara mattar*), cooked
(see p. 210)
1¼ cups / 250 ml Milk
⅛ tsp Sugar
Salt to taste
¼ tsp Mint (*pudina*) powder

**For the spice mix, coarsely
grind (see p. 213) and set aside:**
6 Cashew nuts (*kaju*)
2 tsp / 10 g Poppyseeds
(*khus khus*)
2 Cloves (*laung*)
¼" Cinnamon (*dalchini*) stick
2 Green cardamom pods (*choti
elaichi*), seeds only

METHOD

- Boil 3¾ cups water; add 1 tsp oil and few drops of lemon juice. Add the halved mushrooms and cook on high heat for 20 seconds; drain in a colander and set aside.

- Heat 2-3 tbsp oil in a wok (*kadhai*) for 30 seconds; add the grated onions and ginger and garlic pastes and fry on low heat until the onions are lightly golden and translucent, stirring frequently. Add the red chili powder and the coarsley ground spice mix and mix well.

- Add the whisked yogurt and cook on low heat until the oil separates, stirring continuously.

- Add the cooked peas, mushrooms, milk, sugar, and salt to taste.

- Bring the sauce to a boil on moderate heat and simmer for 2 minutes. Add the mint powder, mix and serve hot.

- Boiling the mushrooms with oil and lemon juice for 20 seconds helps to retain their succulence and natural color.
- Do not over-sauté the onions, as this will alter the color of the sauce.

THIS MILDLY-
SPICED SAUCE BASE, WITH
DELICATE MINT OVERTONES,
CAN ALSO BE TEAMED WITH
PANEER, CORN, OR A MEDLEY
OF VEGETABLES.

• Add the peas and remaining ingredients just before you plan to
serve this dish, so that the peas retain their fresh, green color.

PETITE POTATOES À LA FENUGREEK
Methi Aloo Bahaar

INGREDIENTS

1½ tbsp / 25 ml Mustard oil (*sarson ka tel*)

A pinch Asafoetida (*hing*)

½ tsp / 2½ g Cumin (*jeera*) seeds

3 (tightly-packed) cups Fenugreek (*methi*) leaves, chopped, washed, dried on paper towel

A pinch Sugar

20 / 500 g Baby potatoes, boiled, peeled (see p. 208)

¾ tsp / 3¾ g Red chili powder

2 tsp / 10 g Coriander (*dhaniya*) powder

1/8 tsp Dried mango powder (*amchur*)

Salt to taste

METHOD

• Heat 1½ tbsp mustard oil in a pan for 30 seconds; add the asafoetida and cumin seeds.

• Add the fenugreek leaves and sugar; cook, uncovered, on moderate heat until the moisture dries up, stirring frequently.

• Lower heat and add the peeled baby potatoes; mix. Add the red chili, coriander and dried mango powders, and salt to taste. Sauté for 2 minutes on high heat, stirring frequently. Serve hot.

THE MUCH-LOVED AND VERSATILE POTATO FINDS DELICIOUS COMARADERIE WITH THE FLAVORFUL FENUGREEK LEAVES AND SMOKY MUSTARD OIL.

• This recipe can also be made with 1 lb / 500 g of large, boiled potatoes, peeled and cut into 1" pieces.

• Any vegetable oil can be used instead of mustard oil.

EXOTIC VEGETABLE TRIO
Tirangi Chilgoza Sabzi

THIS COLORFUL VEGETABLE MEDLEY IS INFUSED WITH THE FLAVORS OF THE MEDITERRANEAN, WHILE MAINTAINING ITS UNIQUE INDIAN SPICE SIGNATURE.

INGREDIENTS

1 medium / 200 g Zucchini, cut into ½"-thick semi-circles
Refined vegetable oil for cooking
12 / 200 g Baby potatoes, boiled (see p. 208)
7 oz / 200 g Baby onions (*chotte pyaz*), peeled
A pinch Asafoetida (*hing*)
½ tsp / 2½ g Cumin (*jeera*) seeds
½ tsp / 2½ g Red chili powder
1½ tsp / 7½ g Coriander (*dhaniya*) powder
¼ tsp *Garam masala* powder (see p. 214)
¼ tsp Dried mango powder (*amchur*)
Salt to taste
2 tbsp / 8 g Finely-chopped cilantro (*dhaniya*) leaves
1 tbsp / 10 g Pine nuts (*chilgoza*)

METHOD

- **For the zucchini,** heat 1 tbsp oil in a pan for 30 seconds; add the zucchini pieces and sauté on moderate heat until light golden brown on both sides.

- **For the baby potatoes,** peel and cut the boiled baby potatoes lengthwise. Heat 1 tbsp oil in a pan for 30 seconds and add the potato halves, cut-side down, and fry on moderate heat until light golden brown. Remove and set aside.

- **For the baby onions,** heat 1 tbsp oil in a pan for 30 seconds; add the baby onions and sauté on moderate heat until light golden brown, stirring frequently. Remove and set aside.

- Heat 1 tbsp oil in a pan for 30 seconds; add the asafoetida, cumin seeds, sautéed baby onions, baby potatoes, and zucchini pieces. Add the red chili, coriander, *garam masala* and dried mango powders, salt to taste, and cilantro leaves; mix. Sauté the vegetables for a minute on high heat, stirring frequently.

- Transfer to a serving dish, sprinkle pine nuts on top, and serve immediately.

- It is important to sauté the vegetables separately, as the cooking time is different for each one.

- Pine nuts may be substituted with skinned peanuts (see p. 215).

CAULIFLOWER AU GRATIN INDIEN
Cheesy Gobi Bake

INGREDIENTS

1 medium / 500 g Cauliflower
(*phool gobi*)

2 cups White sauce (see recipe
below)

1 tsp / 5 g Butter (at room
temperature), for greasing

For the spiced white sauce:

1 tbsp / 15 g Butter

¼ tsp Chopped garlic (*lasan*)

1 tbsp / 15 g All-purpose flour
(*maida*)

2 cups / 400 ml Milk (at room
temperature), fresh

Salt to taste

Black peppercorns (*sabut kali
mirch*), freshly ground, to taste

¼ tsp Sugar

1 oz / 25 g Grated cheese, such
as cheddar or colby

2 tbsp / 8 g Finely-chopped
cilantro (*dhaniya*) leaves

2 tbsp / 20 g Peanuts
(*moongphalli*), skinned, coarsely
crushed (see p. 215)

1 tsp / 5 g Green chili paste
(see p. 206)

For the topping:

2 oz / 50 g Cheddar cheese,
grated

1 Salted cracker, finely crushed

THIS HEARTY
CASSEROLE HAS A
DISTINCT INDIAN FLAVOR
THAT COMES FROM THE
FRESH CILANTRO LEAVES,
PEANUTS, AND GREEN
CHILI, WHICH COMBINE
DELICIOUSLY WITH THE
CAULIFLOWER.

• Take care not to overcook the cauliflower, as the florets will lose
their crunch.

METHOD

- Cut the cauliflower into 1" florets (to make 3 cups). Boil 5 cups water, add the cauliflower florets, and cook for 2 minutes. Drain in a colander and set aside.

- **For the spiced white sauce,** heat 1 tbsp butter in a wok (*kadhai*) for 30 seconds; add the garlic and all-purpose flour and cook on moderate heat for 20 seconds, stirring continuously.

- Turn off the heat, add the milk, salt, and black pepper to taste.

- Add the sugar and grated cheese; mix well. Turn the heat back on and bring the milk-cheese mixture to a boil, stirring continuously.

- Turn off the heat after the first boil and stir in the cauliflower florets, cilantro leaves, crushed peanuts, and green chili paste.

- Grease an 8" × 8" baking dish with 1 tsp butter and preheat the oven to 350°F / 180°C. Transfer the cauliflower mixture to the baking dish and evenly sprinkle the topping ingredients on top.

- Once the oven has preheated for about 10 minutes, bake the cauliflower dish for 15-25 minutes or until the top is lightly browned. Serve hot.

- If you plan to prepare this dish in advance, make sure it isn't more than 3 hours before baking, as the milk tends to curdle on account of the cheese.

AS 'N' CHEESE CASSEROLE
Mattar Paneer Francisi

INGREDIENTS

For the white sauce:
2 tbsp / 30 g Butter
2 leveled tbsp / 20 g
All-purpose flour (*maida*)
3 cups / 600 ml Milk (at room temperature)
Salt and freshly-ground black peppercorns, to taste
½ tsp / 2½ g Sugar
2 oz / 40 g Grated cheese, such as cheddar or colby

For the layers:
4 large / 600 g Potatoes, boiled (see p. 208)
Salt to taste
Freshly-ground black pepper (*sabut kali mirch*), to taste
2 tbsp / 8 g Finely-chopped

cilantro (*dhaniya*) or parsley leaves
1 tbsp / 15 ml Refined vegetable oil
½ lb / 250 g Paneer (see p. 204), cut into ½" slices
1½ cups / 225 g Green peas (*hara mattar*), cooked (see p. 210)
1 tbsp Finely-chopped celery stalk (see p. 211)
2 tbsp Bell pepper (*Shimla mirch*) pieces, ¼" in size
1 tsp / 5 g Butter (at room temperature), for greasing

For the topping:
2 oz / 50 g Cheddar cheese, grated
1 Salted cracker, finely crushed

METHOD

- **For the white sauce,** heat 2 tbsp butter in a wok (*kadhai*) for 30 seconds; add all-purpose flour and cook on moderate heat for 20 seconds, stirring continuously.

- Turn off the heat, add milk, salt and black pepper to taste, sugar, and grated cheese; mix well.

- Bring the milk-cheese mixture to a boil, stirring continuously. Turn off the heat and divide the white sauce into ½ cup and 2½ cup portions; set aside.

- **For the potato layer,** peel and coarsely mash the boiled potatoes; mix with salt and freshly ground black pepper to taste, finely-chopped cilantro leaves, and ½ cup of the white sauce; set aside.

- **For the paneer and peas layer,** heat 1 tbsp oil in a pan for 30 seconds and sauté the paneer slices on moderate heat until light golden brown on both sides. Remove and cut into ½" cubes (see p. 205)

- Mix 2½ cups of the white sauce with the paneer cubes, cooked peas, chopped celery, and bell pepper pieces; set aside.

- **To assemble,** grease an 8" x 8" baking dish with 1 tsp butter and preheat the oven to 350°F / 180°C. Spoon in the potato layer and flatten using the underside of a spoon.

- Arrange the paneer and peas layer evenly on top of the potato layer. Sprinkle on the grated cheddar cheese, followed by the cracker crumbs.

- Once the oven has preheated for about 10 minutes, bake the casserole for 15-25 minutes or until the top is lightly browned. Serve hot.

PANEER LENDS THIS DELICIOUS CASSEROLE A DISTINCTIVE INDIAN FLAVOR. ENJOY IT WITH A BAGUETTE OR GARLIC BREAD AT LUNCH OR DINNER.

- Always use room-temperature or cold milk for the white sauce, as adding warm milk will immediately make the flour lumpy.

• The white sauce should not be prepared more than 3 hours ahead of baking the casserole, as the reaction between the milk and cheese might curdle the mixture.

CORN FLORENTINE
Palak Makai Firangi

INGREDIENTS

For the vegetables:
2 (tightly-packed) cups Spinach (*palak*), chopped, washed
¼ tsp Sugar
2 tsp Refined vegetable oil
1 cup / 150 g Sweet corn (*makai*) kernels
2 oz / 50 g Baby corn (*chotte bhutte*), cut into ¼" slanted pieces (½ cup)

For the white sauce:
1 tbsp / 15 g Butter
1 leveled tbsp / 10 g All-purpose flour (*maida*)
1½ cups / 300 ml Milk, fresh
Salt to taste
Freshly-ground black peppercorns (*sabut kali mirch*) to taste
1 oz / 25 g Cheddar cheese, grated
¼ tsp Sugar

To assemble:
1 tsp / 5 g Butter (at room temperature), for greasing
1 oz /25 g Cheddar cheese, grated
1 Salted cracker, finely crushed

METHOD

- **For the spinach,** heat a pan for 30 seconds; add the chopped spinach and ¼ tsp sugar and cook, covered, on moderate heat for a minute. Remove from the pan and set aside to cool.

- **For the corn kernels and baby corns,** heat the oil in a pan for 30 seconds, add the sweet corn kernels and baby corn; cook, covered, on moderate heat for 2 minutes, stirring occasionally. Remove and set aside.

- **For the white sauce,** heat 1 tbsp butter in a wok (*kadhai*) for 30 seconds; add the flour and cook on moderate heat for 20 seconds, stirring continuously.

- Turn off the heat, add the milk, salt and black pepper to taste, grated cheese, and sugar; mix well. Turn the heat back on and bring the white sauce to a boil, stirring continuously; set aside.

- **To assemble,** squeeze the spinach by hand to remove any excess water and add to the white sauce; mix well.

- Now add the cooked sweet corn kernels and baby corn and mix.

- Grease a 6" x 6" baking dish with 1 tsp butter and preheat the oven to 350°F / 180°C. Pour in the mixture. Sprinkle the grated cheddar cheese on top, followed by the cracker crumbs.

- Once the oven has preheated for about 10 minutes, bake the casserole for 15-25 minutes or until the top is lightly browned. Serve hot.

> PACKED WITH WHOLESOME GOODNESS, THIS CRUNCHY CORN AND SPINACH CASSEROLE IS A POPULAR CONTINENTAL ADDITION TO INDIAN MENUS.

- For best results, ensure you preheat the oven before baking and bake the casserole just before you plan to serve.

• It is important to squeeze out any excess water after cooking the spinach, otherwise it will dilute the white sauce.

RICE & BREADS

THREE-ONION PILAF
Pulao Teen Pyaza

Serves: 2-4

INGREDIENTS

1-2 tbsp / 15-30 g Clarified butter (*ghee*)
1" Cinnamon (*dalchini*) stick
2 Black cardamom pods (*badi elaichi*)
2 medium / 150 g Onions, cut into long slices
1 cup / 100 g Baby onions, peeled
1 cup / 175 g Basmati rice, washed, soaked in plenty of water for 30 minutes, drained
Salt to taste
1 cup / 60 g Finely-chopped scallions (*hare pyaz ke patte*) (¾ cup + ¼ cup)

METHOD

• Heat the clarified butter for 30 seconds in a pan; add the cinnamon stick, black cardamom pods, and onion slices; sauté for a minute on moderate heat, stirring continuously.

• Add the baby onions and sauté on moderate heat until light golden brown, stirring continuously. Add the drained rice, 2 cups / 475 ml water, and salt to taste; mix gently and bring the mixture to a boil. Continue to cook, covered, on low heat, until the water is absorbed and the rice is completely cooked.

• Add ¾ cup scallions, mix gently, and transfer to a serving dish.

• Garnish with ¼ cup scallions and serve immediately.

THE CRUNCH OF THE BABY ONIONS, ALONG WITH THE SUBTLE FLAVORS OF CINNAMON AND CARDAMOM MAKE THIS PILAF A UNIQUE CELEBRATION OF FLAVOR AND TEXTURE.

• Soaking the rice helps it to cook evenly.
• Stir the rice occasionally; stirring too much while cooking may break the grains.
• To get long, separated grains, always cook the rice on low heat after it comes to a boil. Cooking on high heat may cause the water to evaporate before the rice is fully cooked.

LOTUS STEM PILAF
Kamal Kakdi Pulao

INGREDIENTS

¼ lb / 125 g Lotus stems (*kamal kakdi*), cut into 1" slanted pieces (see p. 209)
1-2 tbsp / 15-30 g Clarified butter (*ghee*)
2 medium / 150 g Onions, cut into medium cubes
1 tsp / 5 g Ginger (*adrak*) paste (see p. 206)
½ tsp / 2½ g Garlic (*lasan*) paste (see p. 206)
½ tsp / 2½ g Green chili paste (see p. 206)
½ tsp / 2½ g Red chili powder
⅛ tsp Turmeric (*haldi*) powder
3 medium / 225 g Tomatoes, puréed (see p. 213)
1 cup / 175 g Basmati rice, washed, soaked in plenty of water for 30 minutes, drained
Salt to taste

For the spice mix, coarsely grind (see p. 213) and set aside:
2 Black cardamom pods (*badi elaichi*), seeds only
15 Black peppercorns (*sabut kali mirch*)
6 Cloves (*laung*)
½" Cinnamon (*dalchini*) stick

To garnish:
½ cup / 30 g Finely-chopped scallions (*hare pyaz ke patte*)
2 tbsp / 8 g Finely-chopped cilantro (*dhaniya*) leaves

METHOD

- Pressure-cook the lotus stem pieces with 2 cups / 475 ml water to one whistle and turn off the heat. When the pressure drops, remove the lid (see p. 209). (Alternatively, cook in soup pot until tender.) Drain and set aside.

- Heat the clarified butter in a pan for 30 seconds; add the freshly-ground spice mix, onion cubes, ginger, garlic, and green chili pastes and fry on moderate heat until light brown, stirring continuously. Add the red chili and turmeric powders and mix. Add the puréed tomatoes and cook on moderate heat for 2 minutes, stirring often to prevent sticking.

- Add the lotus stem pieces and cook for a minute. Add the rice, 2 cups / 475 ml water and salt to taste; mix gently.

- Bring the rice mixture to a boil and cook, covered, on low heat, until the water is absorbed and the rice is completely cooked. Serve garnished with scallion and cilantro.

THIS AROMATIC RICE DISH COMBINES THE NATURAL CRUNCHINESS OF LOTUS STEM AND SCALLIONS WITH A DELICIOUS MEDLEY OF SPICES.

- The peeled lotus stem pieces measure 1¼ cups.

- It is important to pre-cook the lotus stem pieces for this recipe, as they will not cook fully if added raw.

RICE-YOGURT MEDLEY
Thair Saadam

INGREDIENTS
2 cups / 400 g Yogurt (*dahi*)
¼-½ cup / 50-100 ml Milk,
at room temperature
Salt to taste
2 cups Cooked basmati /
short-grain rice (see p. 216)
2 tbsp Pomegranate seeds
(*anar ke dane*), to garnish

For the tempering:
1 tbsp / 15 ml Refined
vegetable oil
2 tsp / 10 g Husked
split Bengal gram (*chana dal*)
1 tsp / 5 g Husked
split black gram (*urad dal*)
A pinch Asafoetida (*hing*)
½ tsp / 2½ g Mustard
seeds (*rai*)
2 Dried red chilies (*sookhi lal
mirch*), broken
10-15 Curry leaves (*kadhi patta*)

METHOD
• Whisk the yogurt with sufficient milk to a creamy, medium-thick consistency; add salt to taste and mix.

• Gently mix the lukewarm, cooked rice with the whisked yogurt mixture and transfer to a serving dish

• **For the tempering,** heat 1 tbsp oil in a tempering ladle for 30 seconds; add the lentils and sauté on moderate heat until light brown, mixing continuously. Add the asafoetida and mustard seeds. When the mustard seeds splutter, add the broken dried red chilies and curry leaves, mix and immediately pour over the rice and yogurt mixture.

• Garnish with pomegranate seeds and serve immediately. Refrigerate any leftovers.

IN
MOST SOUTH
INDIAN HOMES, THIS
RICE DISH IS SERVED AS A
HEALTHY FINALE TO A MEAL.
IN THE SOUTHERN STATE OF
TAMIL NADU IT IS KNOWN
AS THAIR SAADAM.

• To make 2 cups of cooked rice, use ²/₃ cup (125 g) of raw rice.

• To get the right texture, ensure that the rice is lukewarm, and not hot, when mixing in the yogurt.

LEMON YELLOW RICE
Namkeen Nimbu Chawal

INGREDIENTS
1½ tbsp / 25 ml Refined vegetable oil
2 tsp / 10 g Husked split Bengal gram (*chana dal*)
1 tsp / 5 g Husked split black gram (*urad dal*)
½ tsp / 2½ g Mustard seeds (*rai*)
2 Dried red chilies (*sookhi lal mirch*)
1 Green chili, slit
⅛ tsp Turmeric (*haldi*) powder
10-15 Curry leaves (*kadhi patta*)
2 cups Cooked basmati / short-grain rice (see p. 216)
Salt to taste
1 tbsp / 15 ml Lemon juice (*nimbu ka ras*)
2 tbsp / 20 g Peanuts (*moongphalli*), deep-fried (see p. 215) (1 tbsp + 1 tbsp)
2 tbsp / 8 g Finely-chopped cilantro (*dhaniya*) leaves (1 tbsp + 1 tbsp)

METHOD
• Heat the oil in a wok (*kadhai*) for 30 seconds; add both the husked split Bengal gram and split black gram and sauté on moderate heat until light brown, stirring continuously. Add the mustard seeds and when they splutter, add the dried red chilies, slit green chili, turmeric powder, and curry leaves; mix.

• Lower the heat and immediately add the cooked rice (at room temperature) and mix gently. Add salt to taste and lemon juice.

• Add 1 tbsp deep-fried peanuts and 1 tbsp cilantro leaves; mix gently on moderate heat for 2 minutes.

• Transfer to a serving dish and serve hot, garnished with remaining deep-fried peanuts and cilantro leaves.

THIS SIMPLE, TANGY RICE DISH IS A SOUTH INDIAN SPECIALTY AND IS A STAPLE PREPARATION DURING THE HARVEST FESTIVAL OF PONGAL.

• To avoid a bitter aftertaste, always follow the specified cooking time after adding lemon juice.

• This recipe is a great way to use leftover, cooked, plain rice.

SPINACH PILAF
Palak Pulao

INGREDIENTS

1 lb / 500 g Spinach (*palak*)
½ tsp / 2½ g Sugar
2 tbsp / 30 ml Refined vegetable oil
1 large / 100 g Onion, cut into medium cubes
Salt to taste
¼ tsp Red chili powder
1 large / 100 g Firm tomato, cut into medium cubes
1 tbsp / 15 g Clarified butter (*ghee*)
½ tsp / 2½ g Cumin (*jeera*) seeds
1 cup / 175 g Basmati rice, washed, soaked in plenty of water for 30 minutes, drained
1 tbsp / 15 ml Milk
1 tbsp / 15 ml Heavy cream

For the spice mix, coarsely grind (see p. 213) and set aside:
1 Black cardamom (*badi elaichi*), seeds only
4 Cloves (*laung*)
5 Black peppercorns (*sabut kali mirch*)
¼" Cinnamon (*dalchini*) stick

METHOD

• **For the spinach,** discard the hard stems of the spinach, and finely chop the rest of the greens. Wash and drain the chopped spinach in a colander. Heat a pan for 30 seconds; add the spinach and ½ tsp sugar and cook, covered, on moderate heat for 2 minutes.

• Uncover, cool, and coarsely purée in a blender / food processor with 2 cups / 400 ml water and set aside (this purée is used to cook the rice).

• Heat 1 tbsp oil in a pan for 30 seconds; add the onion cubes and sauté on moderate heat until lightly golden in color, stirring continuously. Add salt to taste, mix, and set aside.

• Heat 1 tbsp oil in a pan for 30 seconds; add the red chili powder, tomato cubes, and salt to taste. Cook on high heat for 30 seconds, stirring continuously; set aside.

• Heat 1 tbsp clarified butter in a pan for 30 seconds; add the cumin seeds and drained rice. Sauté on high heat for 30 seconds, mixing gently. Add the puréed spinach and salt to taste; bring the mixture to a boil on moderate heat. Cook, covered, on low heat until the rice is parboiled.

• Now add the milk, heavy cream, and freshly-ground spice mix; stir gently. Continue to cook, covered, on low heat, until the water is absorbed and the rice is completely cooked. Gently mix in the sautéed onion and tomato cubes and serve immediately.

THIS VIBRANTLY COLORED RICE WILL PIQUE YOUR PALATE WITH ITS SUBTLE SPICE, THE FULL-BODIED FLAVOR OF THE SPINACH, AND THE CRUNCH OF THE TOMATOES AND ONIONS

• Drain the chopped spinach thoroughly after washing to obtain a thick purée.

- After cooking, keep the pilaf covered with a mesh so that the spinach retains its green color. To reheat, use a microwave.

SAFFRON VEGETABLE PILAF
Zafrani Tahari

INGREDIENTS

$^1/_8$ tsp Saffron (*kesar*), soaked in 2 tsp hot milk for 5 minutes

¼ cup / 50 g Yogurt cheese (hung yogurt; *chakka*, see p. 202)

½ tsp / 2½ g Green chili paste (see p. 206)

½ tsp / 2½ g Garlic (*lasan*) paste (see p. 206)

Refined vegetable oil for deep-frying

2 medium / 150 g Potatoes, peeled, diced, immersed in water, pat-dried with paper towel

¾ cup Cauliflower (*phool gobi*) florets, ½" in size

10 French / Green beans, cut into 1" slanted pieces

1 large / 100 g Onion, cut into long slices

1 tbsp / 15 g Clarified butter (*ghee*)

2 Green cardamom pods (*choti elaichi*), seeds only, ground (see p. 219)

1 cup / 175 g Basmati rice, washed, soaked in plenty of water for 30 minutes, drained

Salt to taste

For the spice mix, coarsely grind (see p. 213) and set aside:

¼" Cinnamon (*dalchini*) stick

1 Black cardamom (*badi elaichi*), seeds only

4 Cloves (*laung*)

8 Black peppercorns (*sabut kali mirch*)

METHOD

- Using a mortar and pestle, mash the saffron and milk mixture and set aside.

- Mix the yogurt cheese with the freshly-ground spice mix and the green chili and garlic pastes; set aside.

- Pour oil to the depth of 1" in a wok (*kadhai*) and heat until moderately hot. Deep-fry the potatoes in moderately-hot oil until three-quarters cooked, turning occasionally. Add the cauliflower florets and continue to fry in moderately-hot oil, until florets are light brown, turning occasionally. Add the cut beans and deep-fry for a minute. Remove the fried vegetables, drain on absorbent paper towel, and set aside.

- In the same hot oil, deep-fry the onion slices on high heat until golden brown, turning frequently. Remove, drain on an absorbent paper towel, and set aside.

- The diced potatoes are immersed in water to prevent discoloration.
- Follow the order given for frying the vegetables, as each has a different cooking time.

- Heat 1 tbsp clarified butter in a pan for 30 seconds; add the green cardamom powder and drained rice; mix gently on moderate heat for 30 seconds. Add 2 cups / 400 ml water and salt to taste. Bring the rice mixture to a boil and cook, covered, on low heat until the rice is three-quarters cooked.

- Add the saffron milk and mix well.

- Add the spiced yogurt mixture.

- Add the deep-fried vegetables and onions and mix gently. Continue to cook, covered, on low heat, until the water is absorbed and the rice is completely cooked.

- Serve hot with plain or Chili-Garlic Yogurt (p. 156).

THE ROBUST FLAVORS OF THE SPICED VEGETABLES ARE COMPLEMENTED BY THE DELICATE AROMA OF SAFFRON IN THIS WHOLESOME, ONE-DISH MEAL.

TANGY EGGPLANT PILAF
Pulao Baingan Bahaar

INGREDIENTS

1 cup / 175 g Basmati rice, washed, soaked in plenty of water for 30 minutes, drained
½ oz / 15 g Tamarind (*imli*)
½ lb / 250 g Tender baby eggplants (*chotte baingan*)
Refined vegetable oil for deep-frying
Salt to taste
½ tsp / 2½ g *Garam masala* powder (see p. 214)
2 tsp / 10 g White sesame (*safed til*) seeds, toasted (see p. 215)
2 tbsp Green peas (*hara mattar*), cooked (see p. 210)
2 tbsp / 8 g Finely-chopped cilantro (*dhaniya*) leaves

For the seasoning:
2 tbsp / 30 ml Refined vegetable oil
⅛ tsp Asafoetida (*hing*)
½ tsp / 2½ g Mustard seeds (*rai*)
1 tsp / 5 g Ginger (*adrak*) paste (see p. 206)
1 tsp / 5 g Green chili paste (see p. 206)
4 Dried red chilies (*sookhi lal mirch*), broken
10 Curry leaves (*kadhi patta*)
¼ tsp Turmeric (*haldi*) powder
½ tsp / 2½ g Red chili powder

METHOD

• Boil 7½ cups water, add the rice, and bring to a boil. Cook, covered, on low heat until the rice is cooked. Drain in a colander and set aside (see p. 216).

• Soak the tamarind in ½ cup hot water for 30 minutes. Mash and strain into a bowl, discarding seeds and any other residue. Set the tamarind extract aside.

• Trim the eggplant stems. Slit half of the eggplants vertically, three-quarters of the way down, keeping the vegetable intact at the stem. Slit the remaining eggplants in half vertically.

• Pour oil to the depth of 1" in a wok (*kadhai*) and heat. Deep-fry the eggplants in hot oil, until the skin crinkles slightly and the flesh turns light golden brown. Remove, drain on an absorbent paper towel, and set aside.

• **For the seasoning**, heat 2 tbsp oil in a wok (*kadhai*) for 30 seconds; add the asafoetida and mustard seeds. When the mustard seeds splutter, lower the heat and add the ginger and green chili pastes, dried red chilies, curry leaves, turmeric, and red chili powder; mix. Add the tamarind extract and cook on low heat until the oil separates.

• Add the deep-fried eggplants and mix. Add the cooked rice, salt to taste, *garam masala* powder, and sesame seeds; mix well.

• Add the cooked peas and cilantro leaves. Cook for 2 minutes on high heat, stirring gently; serve hot.

FROM THE TENDER EGGPLANTS AND THE NUTTY SESAME SEEDS, TO THE TANGY TAMARIND AND THE FIERY GARAM MASALA, THIS PILAF TAKES YOU ON A DELICIOUS, SPICE-FILLED CULINARY JOURNEY.

• Leftover, plain, cooked rice can be used to make this dish.

• Slit the eggplants just before deep-frying, to avoid discoloration and a slightly bitter aftertaste.

• Deep-fry the eggplants in hot oil to prevent them from absorbing too much oil on account of their sponge-like texture.

HEARTY JACKFRUIT RICE 'N' SPICE
Kacche Kathal Ki Biryani

INGREDIENTS
½ cup / 100 g Soft yogurt
cheese (hung yogurt; *chakka*,
see p. 202)
2 tsp / 10 g Mint (*pudina*) paste
(see p. 207)
Refined vegetable oil for
deep-frying
2 cups / 200 g Tender, skinned
raw jackfruit (*kathal*), cut into
1" pieces (see p. 209)
1½ tbsp / 25 g Clarified butter
(*ghee*)
1 Bay leaf (tej p*atta*)
2 medium / 150 g Onions,
cut into long slices
2 tsp / 10 g Ginger (*adrak*)
paste (see p. 206)
1 tsp / 10 g Garlic (*lasan*) paste
(see p. 206)
1 cup / 175 g Basmati rice,
washed, soaked in plenty of
water for 30 minutes, drained
Salt to taste
2 tbsp / 8 g Finely-chopped
cilantro (*dhaniya*) leaves

For the spice mix, coarsely grind (see p. 213) and set aside:
4 Green cardamom pods
(*choti elaichi*), seeds only
1 Black cardamom (*badi elaichi*),
seeds only
1" Cinnamon (*dalchini*) stick
15 Black peppercorns
(*sabut kali mirch*)

METHOD
• Mix the soft yogurt cheese with the freshly-ground spice mix and mint paste; set aside.

• Pour oil to the depth of 1" in a wok (*kadhai*) and heat until moderately hot. Deep-fry the jackfruit pieces in hot oil until light golden brown. Remove, drain on paper towel, and set aside.

• Heat 1½ tbsp clarified butter in a pan for 30 seconds; add the bay leaf, onions, and ginger and garlic pastes; sauté on moderate heat for a minute, stirring continuously. Add the deep-fried jackfruit, drained rice, 2 cups / 400 ml water, and salt to taste. Bring the mixture to a boil and cook, covered, on low heat until the rice is three-quarters cooked.

• Now gently stir the spiced yogurt cheese mixture into the rice. Continue to cook covered on low heat, until the water is absorbed and the rice is completely cooked.

• Garnish with cilantro leaves and serve hot with Chili-Garlic Yogurt (p. 156) or plain yogurt.

• Pick raw jackfruit that is young and tender, as the seeds of the older fruit have a hard cover and cannot be used in this dish.

THE
UNIQUE FLAVOR
OF JACKFRUIT PERFECTLY
COMPLEMENTS THE SPICED
YOGURT CHEESE AND THE
HEARTY BASMATI RICE.

• Make sure you use the same measuring cup to measure all ingredients.

WATER CHESTNUT & ASPARAGUS PILAF
Singhada Shatwar Pulao

INGREDIENTS

½ lb / 250 g Asparagus
(*shatwar*)
1 tbsp / 15 g Butter
¼ tsp Black peppercorns (*sabut kali mirch*), coarsely ground
1 cup / 60 g Finely-chopped scallions (*hare pyaz ke patte*)
20 / 500 g Raw water chestnuts (*singhada*), peeled
1 cup / 175 g Basmati rice, washed, soaked in plenty of water for 30 minutes, drained
Salt to taste

METHOD

• Cut 1" off the asparagus heads and set aside for the garnish. If necessary, shave the remaining spear with a sharp knife or asparagus peeler. Cut off and disgard the hard ends of the asparagus spears and cut the rest into ¼" discs.

• Heat ½ tsp butter in a pan for 20 seconds; add the asparagus heads and sauté on moderate heat for 30 seconds. Remove and set aside.

• In a separate pan, heat the remaining butter for 30 seconds; add the black pepper, scallions, asparagus discs, and water chestnuts. Sauté for 30 seconds on moderate heat, stirring continuously.

• Add the drained rice, 2 cups / 400 ml water, and salt to taste; mix gently. Bring to a boil and cook, covered, on low heat, until the water is absorbed and the rice is completely cooked.

• Serve hot, garnished with the sautéed asparagus heads.

THE EXOTIC PAIRING OF ASPARAGUS AND WATER CHESTNUTS COMES TOGETHER IN THIS UNUSUAL, MILDLY-SPICED PILAF.

• This dish calls for tender, green asparagus. Do not use the white or purple variety.

• If fresh water chestnuts are not available, use canned, whole water chestnuts, after draining.

HANDKERCHIEF FOLDS
Makhmali Roomali Roti

INGREDIENTS

2 cups / 250 g All-purpose flour (*maida*)
1 tbsp / 15 g Whole-wheat flour (*atta*)
¼ tsp Baking soda
½ tsp / 2½ g Salt
2 tbsp / 30 g Yogurt (*dahi*)
2 tbsp / 30 ml Heavy cream
½ cup / 60 g (approx) All-purpose flour, for dusting

METHOD

- Sieve together all-purpose flour, whole-wheat flour, baking soda, and salt. Add the yogurt and heavy cream.

- Add sufficient water to knead into a very soft dough. Cover the dough with a damp cloth and leave to stand for 30 minutes. Invert a shallow wok (*kadhai*) over a burner and heat on moderate heat until hot.

- Meanwhile, divide the dough into 10 equal portions and shape into balls. Dust each ball with some all-purpose flour, flatten with your palm and, using a rolling pin, roll out as thinly as possible on a rolling board (*chakla*), dusting often to avoid sticking.

- Carefully lift the *roomali roti* off the rolling board with one hand and flip to your other hand. Flip 3-4 times carefully elongating the *roti* to about 11" in diameter.

- Place on the heated, inverted wok and, after 20 seconds, flip by hand.

- Gently flip at intervals of 20 seconds, until light brown spots appear on both sides of the *roti*.

- Remove, and fold or roll the *roti*.

- Repeat the process, adjusting the heat while you roll out the next *roti* to ensure the wok stays at the right temperature.

- Serve immediately.

   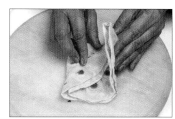

- The dough for this particular Indian bread should be very soft and prepared fresh.

- Adding a little whole-wheat flour makes it easier to roll out the naturally elastic flour dough.

THE
WORD *ROOMALI*
HAS ITS ORIGINS IN
THE HINDI WORD *ROOMAL*,
WHICH MEANS HANDKERCHIEF.
IN INDIAN RESTAURANTS, MAKING
ROOMALIS CALLS FOR A SPECIALIZED
CHEF, REVERED IN THE KITCHEN
FOR HIS TOSSING SKILLS.

- This bread is traditionally cooked on a large, inverted, shallow wok (*kadhai*).

- Handkerchief Folds are best enjoyed with *tikka* and kebab dishes as well as Black Velvet Lentils (p. 86).

LAYERED CRISPY BREAD
Lachchedaar Tandoori Paratha

INGREDIENTS
2 cups / 250 g Whole-wheat flour (*atta*)
½ tsp / 2½ g Salt
1 tsp / 5 g Baking powder
¼ cup / 50 ml Milk (at room temperature)
2-3 tbsp / 30-45 g Clarified butter (*ghee*), to apply
½ cup / 60 g (approx) Whole-wheat flour, for dusting
2-3 tsp / 10-15 g Mint (*pudina*) powder, to sprinkle

METHOD
• Sieve together the whole-wheat flour and salt. Make a well in the center of the sieved flour, add the baking powder, and pour in the milk. Wait for a minute or two until the surface of the milk bubbles and mix together.

• Add sufficient water to knead into a medium dough. Cover with a damp cloth and let it stand for an hour.

• Divide the dough into equal portions, shape into balls, and roll out each ball into a 5" disc. Apply ¼ tsp clarified butter and sprinkle ½ tsp whole-wheat flour evenly over the discs.

• Fold each disc from one end to another forming 1" pleats.

• Lay the pleated rectangle horizontally and fold 1" of the left end of the dough inwards.

• Holding the right end, coil the entire pleated rectangle around the center fold, making concentric circles.

• Dust with whole-wheat flour and roll out again into a 3.5" disc (*paratha*).

• Place a gas tandoor or a large inverted soup pot over the burner and heat until hot. Test by sprinkling a little water; it should sizzle and evaporate immediately. Moisten your palm with water and gently pat the *paratha*. If using a pot, flip it right-side up. Stick 3-4 *parathas* to the inner walls of of the gas tandoor / pot (see picture); invert over the burner, and cook on high heat for 1-2 minutes, until light golden brown. The *parathas* will fall once fully cooked. (Alternatively, bake in an oven preheated to 480°F / 250°C.)

• Toast over an open flame for even browning, if required.

• Remove, apply ½ tsp clarified butter to each *paratha*, and sprinkle mint powder on top; serve immediately.

TRADITIONALLY COOKED IN A COAL OR WOOD-FIRED CLAY OVEN, THIS CRISP, UNLEAVENED BREAD MUST BE EATEN PIPING HOT, TOPPED WITH A DOLLOP OF CLARIFIED BUTTER.

• Adding baking powder to the dough helps to make the *parathas* crispier.
• Sprinkling ½ tsp whole-wheat flour on the discs before pleating helps to separate the pleated layers while cooking.

• You can half-cook the *parathas* in advance and store them in the refrigerator, wrapped in foil, for up to 4 days. Just before serving, warm on a griddle, then turn and toast over an open flame.
• This Indian bread is a delicious accompaniment to any Indian entrée.

FENUGREEK MAIZE BREAD
Makka Methi Paratha

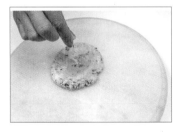

INGREDIENTS

2 leveled cups / 200 g Cornmeal or corn flour (*makke ka atta*)
½ cup / 60 g (approx) Whole-wheat flour (*atta*)
1 tsp / 5 g Salt
A pinch Asafoetida (*hing*)
2 tsp / 10 g Red chili powder
2 (loosely-packed) cups Fenugreek (*methi*) leaves, chopped
½ cup / 60 g (approx) Cornmeal or corn flour, for dusting
Mustard / Refined vegetable oil for cooking

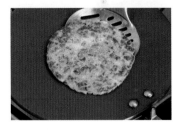

METHOD

• Sieve together the cornmeal or corn flour with whole-wheat flour and salt. Add the asafoetida, red chili powder, and fenugreek leaves.

• Add sufficient water to knead into a medium, smooth dough (neither too hard, nor too soft).

• Divide into 8-10 equal portions, gently knead each portion, and shape into balls.

• Flatten gently with your palm, dust with cornmeal, and roll into 2" discs using a rolling pin.

• Apply ¼ tsp oil and sprinkle cornmeal on the disc.

• Fold into a money bag, flatten and dust lightly with cornmeal or corn flour again.

• Now roll into 5" discs.

• Add ½ tsp oil to a moderately-hot griddle (*tava*); carefully lift and place the disc on it. Shallow-fry each disc until light golden brown on both sides, about 1 minute each side.

• Drizzle 1 tbsp oil on each cooked disc and serve immediately.

THE ADDITION OF FENUGREEK GIVES THIS DELICIOUS FLAT-BREAD A UNIQUE FLAVOR. IT IS TRADITIONALLY SERVED WITH BUTTER AND FRESH, HOMEMADE PICKLE.

• Maize is a winter cereal that has warming properties and is savored during the cold months in north India.

• Since cornmeal (or the slightly finer corn flour) tends to be coarse, re-kneading individual portions of dough makes them easier to roll out.

• This bread can be served with the more elaborate Indian Cheese
Florentine (p. 92) or simply Leafy Green Yogurt (p. 154).

QUESADILLA INDIAN STYLE
Chatpatta Cheese Paratha

INGREDIENTS

For the dough:

½ cup / 60 g Whole-wheat flour (*atta*)
½ cup / 60 g All-purpose flour (*maida*)
¼ tsp Salt
3 tsp / 15 g Butter (at room temperature)
½ cup / 60 g Whole-wheat flour, for dusting
Refined vegetable oil for cooking

For the filling:

12 medium / 125 g Mushrooms (*khumb*), sliced
½ cup Olives (*jaitoon*), sliced
3 oz / 75 g Zucchini, finely chopped (¾ cup)
¼ lb / 100 g Cheddar cheese, grated
½ tsp / 2½ g *Chaat masala* (see p. 214)
1 tbsp / 4 g Finely-chopped cilantro (*dhaniya*) leaves

METHOD

- Sieve together the whole-wheat flour with all-purpose flour and salt; add butter and mix well.

- Add sufficient water to knead into a soft dough. Divide the dough into eight equal portions and shape into balls.

- Dust each ball with whole-wheat flour, flatten gently with your palm, and roll into thin 6" discs, using a rolling pin.

- Place the disc on a moderately-hot griddle (*tava*) and cook for 10 seconds on moderate heat. Flip and cook for another 10 seconds; remove and place in a muslin cloth. Repeat the process for the remaining discs and wrap them all in the muslin cloth.

- Just before serving, mix all the ingredients for the filling and divide into four equal portions.

- Brush a little oil on a moderately-hot griddle. Place a disc on the griddle and evenly spread one portion of filling mixture on the disc. Place another disc over the filling and press gently.

- Cook on low heat, until the bottom surface turns light golden brown. Now brush oil on top and carefully flip; continue to cook on low heat until light golden brown on the other side.

- Remove, cut into four pieces. Repeat with the rest of the dough and filling and serve immediately.

IF YOU PREFER, THE DOUGH CAN BE MADE ENTIRELY WITH WHOLE-WHEAT FLOUR. YOU CAN EXPERIMENT WITH STUFFING INGREDIENTS OF YOUR CHOICE. JUST MAKE SURE TO CHOP / MASH THEM WELL.

- This recipe is an ingenious Indian variation of the Mexican quesadilla and can be enjoyed as part of a main meal or as a delicious party hors d'oeurve.

STUFFED MILLET BREAD
Bajra Bathua Paratha

INGREDIENTS

For the filling:
2 (tightly-packed) cups / 80 g Lambsquarters (*bathua*) leaves
6 medium / 450 g Potatoes, boiled, peeled, grated (see p. 208)
2 tsp / 10 g Finely-chopped Ginger (*adrak*)
2 tsp / 10 g Finely-chopped Green chilies
Salt to taste

For the dough:
2 cups / 200 g Pearl millet flour (*bajre ka atta*)
½ cup / 60 g (approx) Whole-wheat flour (*atta*)
½ tsp / 2½ g Salt
Lukewarm water to prepare the dough
½ cup / 50 g Pearl millet flour, for dusting
Clarified butter (*ghee*), for cooking

METHOD

- **For the filling,** heat a pan for 30 seconds; add the lambsquarters leaves and cook, covered, on moderate heat for a minute.

- Turn off the heat, cool, and squeeze out any water from the leaves.

- Mash the leaves using the back of a spoon and mix with the grated potatoes, ginger, green chilies, and salt to taste. Set aside.

- **For the dough,** sieve together the pearl millet flour, whole-wheat flour, and salt. Add suffiecient lukewarm water to knead into a soft dough. Keep kneading until the dough feels smooth and shows no cracks on the surface.

- Divide the dough into 10-12 equal portions. Take one portion, slightly knead again, shape into a ball, and dust with pearl millet flour.

- Place the ball on a rolling board (*chakla*) and gently flatten with your fingers to a 3" disc; place 1 tbsp of the filling in the center and fold the dough into a moneybag to seal the filling inside.

- Dust with pearl millet flour again, and gently flatten while holding between your palm and fingers.

- Dust the rolling board, place the stuffed disc on it, sprinkle a little pearl millet flour on top, and with your palm, gently press and rotate, increasing the size to a 5" disc.

- Add ½ tsp clarified butter to a moderately-hot griddle (*tava*). Tilt the rolling board, gently lift the disc, and carefully place on the heated griddle, turning the heat to high. After a minute or two, flip using a flat spatula and wait for a minute. Drizzle 2 tsp clarified butter all around the disc; flip and drizzle again with 2 tsp clarified butter. Shallow-fry until light golden brown on both sides, drizzling additional clarified butter, if required. Repeat with the rest of the dough and filling. Serve immediately.

SERVED WITH PLAIN YOGURT AND PICKLE, THIS DELICACY IS ENJOYED AS WINTER COMFORT FOOD, ACCOMPANIED WITH A GENEROUS DOLLOP OF BUTTER AND JAGGERY.

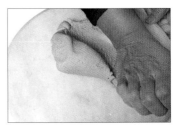

- If you find the disc sticking to the rolling board, use a flat spatula to gently loosen it.

- If you prefer to use a rolling pin instead of your hands, place the stuffed discs between two sheets of plastic wrap or parchment paper before rolling.

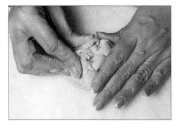   

- Lambsquarters (also called white goosefoot, pigweed, and fat-hen) is in the same family as spinach. If you're unable to find lambsquarters, substitute baby spinach leaves.

- As an alternative to the lambsquarters, you can use 2 tbsp freshly-chopped cilantro leaves and omit the cooking step.

MASALA MAIZE PUFFS
Makke Ki Kachori

Makes: 20

INGREDIENTS

¾ cup / 125 g Husked split black gram (*dhuli urad dal*), soaked in plenty of water for 3 hours, drained
2 cups / 250 g Cornmeal or corn flour (*makke ka atta*)
1 tsp / 5 g Salt
⅛ tsp Asafoetida (*hing*)
½ tsp / 2½ g Red chili powder
½ cup / 60 g (approx) Cornmeal or corn flour, for dusting
Refined vegetable oil, for deep-frying

METHOD

- Grind the soaked black gram with 1 cup / 200 ml water to a smooth paste in a blender / food processor.

- Sieve the cornmeal or corn flour with salt. Add the black gram paste, asafoetida, and red chili powder; mix.

- Knead into a semi-hard, smooth dough with no cracks on the surface. Sprinkle a little water, while kneading, if required. Divide the dough into 20 equal portions and shape into balls. Gently flatten and lightly dust each one with cornmeal or corn flour. Roll into 3½" discs with a rolling pin.

- Pour oil to the depth of 1" in a wok (*kadhai*) and heat until near-smoking point. Lower one disc into the hot oil and gently press the disc with the flat portion (not the sharp edge) of a slotted spoon for about 20 seconds.

- Flip and gently press again until it puffs up. Continue to deep-fry until light golden brown on both sides. Remove and drain on absorbent paper towel. Repeat the process to fry the remaining discs and serve immediately.

THIS FLUFFY, SAVORY BREAD IS A HEARTY ADDITION TO MEALTIMES DURING THE WINTER MONTHS.

- Roll out and deep-fry the discs within 2-3 hours of making the dough, or the husked, split black gram in it will begin to ferment.

- Pair this bread with Classic Curry Trio (p. 112), Leafy Green Yogurt (p. 154), and Chili Pickle in Minutes (p. 158).

LEAFY FENNEL BREAD
Hari Saunfili Roti

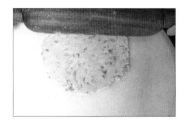

THE UNUSUAL UNION OF SCALLIONS, FENNEL, AND GRAM FLOUR CREATES AN AROMATIC INDIAN BREAD THAT NEEDS NO SPECIAL OCCASION TO BE ENJOYED.

INGREDIENTS
1 cup / 125 g Whole-wheat flour (*atta*)
1 cup / 125 g Gram flour (*besan*)
½ tsp / 2½ g Salt
⅛ tsp Asafoetida (*hing*)
½ tsp / 2½ g Red chili powder
2 tsp / 10 g Fennel (*saunf*) powder
2 tbsp / 30 g Yogurt (*dahi*)
1¼ cups Finely-chopped scallions (*hare pyaz ke patte*)
½ cup / 60 g (approx) Whole-wheat flour, for dusting
1-2 tbsp / 15-30 g Clarified butter (*ghee*)

METHOD
• Sieve together the whole-wheat flour with gram flour and salt. Add the asafoetida, red chili powder, fennel powder, yogurt, and scallions; mix well. Add sufficient water to knead into a semi-hard dough. Cover with a damp cloth and let it stand for 30 minutes.

• Divide the dough into 10-12 equal portions and shape into balls. Dust with whole-wheat flour, flatten gently with your palm, and roll into 4" discs.

• Place each disc on a moderately-hot griddle (*tava*), and cook for 30 seconds. Flip and prick the disc all over with a fork.

• Remove with tongs and toast over an open flame until light golden brown on both sides.

• Smear ½ tsp clarified butter on top and serve immediately.

• To prepare this bread in advance, follow the recipe until the step of pricking with a fork and then wrap the discs in kitchen foil. Just before serving, warm them on a griddle, and toast over an open flame.

ACCOMPANIMENTS

LEAFY GREEN YOGURT
Bathua Raita

Serves: 4-6

INGREDIENTS

1½ (tightly-packed) cups / 60 g
Lambsquarters (*bathua*) leaves
(see p. 148), washed
2 cups / 400 g Yogurt (*dahi*),
strained in a sieve for
20 minutes (see p. 202)
¼ cup / 50 ml Milk, chilled
Salt to taste
¼ tsp Red chili powder,
to garnish

For the tempering:

½ tsp / 2½ g Clarified butter
(*ghee*)
A pinch Asafoetida (*hing*)
½ tsp / 2½ g Cumin (*jeera*)
seeds

METHOD

• Pressure cook the lambsquarters with 2 cups / 475 ml water to
one whistle (or cook in a saucepan until wilted). Cool and drain
in a colander, squeezing out any excess water from the leaves.

• Grate and refrigerate.

• Whisk the strained yogurt with the chilled milk until smooth and
refrigerate.

• Just before serving, **make the tempering**: heat the clarified butter
in a tempering ladle for 30 seconds; add the asafoetida and cumin
seeds. Mix.

• Add the grated lambsquarters and salt to the yogurt; mix and
transfer to a serving dish. Top with the tempering, sprinkle with
red chili powder, and serve.

THIS YOGURT
DELICACY, WITH THE
NATURAL, EARTHY FLAVOR
OF LAMBSQUARTERS IS THE
PERFECT ACCOMPANIMENT
TO WINTER BREADS.

• You can coarsely chop the lambsquarters in a blender / food
processor instead of grating them.

• This dish makes a delicious accompaniment to Fenugreek Maize
Bread (see p. 144) or Masala Maize Puffs (see p. 150).

CORN CHILI YOGURT
Lazeez Makai Raita

Serves: 4-6

INGREDIENTS

1 tsp / 5 ml Refined vegetable oil
¾ cup / 115 g Sweet corn (*makai*) kernels
2 cups / 400 g Yogurt (*dahi*), strained in a fine sieve for 20 minutes (see p. 202)
¼ cup / 50 ml Milk, chilled
1 tsp / 5 g Honey (*shehed*)
Salt to taste

For the tempering:

1 tsp / 5 ml Refined vegetable oil
⅛ tsp Red chili flakes
2 tsp Finely-chopped scallions (*hare pyaz ke patte*)

METHOD

• Heat 1 tsp oil in a pan for 30 seconds; add the sweet corn kernels and sauté on moderate heat for a minute; remove and set aside to cool.

• Whisk the strained yogurt with chilled milk until smooth. Add the sautéed corn kernels, honey, and salt to taste; mix and refrigerate.

• Just before serving, transfer to a serving dish.

• **For the tempering,** heat 1 tsp oil in a tempering ladle for 30 seconds; add the chili flakes and scallions. Mix and pour over the yogurt immediately.

THIS UNUSUAL SIDE DISH GETS ITS SUBTLE HOT-SWEET FLAVOR FROM THE HONEY-CHILI SEASONING.

CHILI-GARLIC YOGURT
Tikha-Lehsuni Raita

RELISHED
FOR ITS HEADY CHILI-
GARLIC FLAVOR, THIS
YOGURT IS USUALLY
SERVED WITH BIRYANIS
AND SPICY PILAFS.

INGREDIENTS
1 tsp / 5 ml Refined
vegetable oil
6 Garlic (*lasan*) cloves
1 tsp / 5 g Finely-chopped
green chilies
2 cups / 400 g Yogurt
(*dahi*), strained for 20 minutes
(see p. 202)
¼ cup / 50 ml Milk, chilled
¼ tsp Red chili powder
Salt to taste
For the tempering:
2 tsp / 10 ml Refined
vegetable oil
1 tsp / 5 g Finely-chopped Garlic
⅛ tsp Red chili flakes
2 tsp Finely-chopped cilantro
(*dhaniya*) leaves
To garnish:
¼ tsp Cumin (*jeera*) powder,
toasted (see p. 214)
2 tsp Finely-chopped cilantro
(*dhaniya*) leaves

METHOD
- Heat 1 tsp oil in a pan for 30 seconds; add the garlic cloves and sauté on moderate heat until light brown. Add the green chilies and mix.

- Remove, cool, and pound to a coarse paste in a mortar and pestle; set aside.

- Whisk the strained yogurt with the chilled milk until smooth. Add the red chili powder, garlic-chili paste, and salt to taste; mix and refrigerate.

- Just before serving, make the tempering: Heat 2 tsp oil in a tempering ladle for 30 seconds; add the chopped garlic and sauté on moderate heat until light brown. Add the red chili flakes and cilantro leaves; mix.

- Transfer the strained yogurt mixture to a serving bowl, top with the tempering, and garnish with toasted cumin powder and cilantro leaves.

- For a less spicy version, omit the green chilies.

- This yogurt dish is served with Saffron Vegetable Pilaf (see p. 132) and Hearty Jackfruit Rice 'n' Spice (see p. 136).

TEMPERED OKRA YOGURT
Tadkedaar Bhindi Raita

A ROBUSTLY FLAVORED YOGURT ACCOMPANIMENT, THIS DELICIOUS RECIPE COMBINES THE CRUNCH OF DEEP-FRIED OKRA WITH THE SHARP FLAVOR OF MUSTARD.

INGREDIENTS

Refined vegetable oil for deep-frying

¼ lb / 100 g Okra (*bhindi*), tender, washed, wiped, heads and tails removed, cut into ⅛" discs

2 cups / 400 g Yogurt (*dahi*), strained for 20 minutes (see p. 202)

¼ cup / 50 ml Milk, chilled

1 tsp / 5 g Cilantro (*dhaniya*) paste (see p. 207)

¼ tsp Green chili paste (see p. 206)

¼ tsp Ginger (*adrak*) paste (see p. 206)

½ tsp / 2½ g Mustard (*sarson*) powder

Salt to taste

For the tempering:

2 tsp / 10 ml Refined vegetable oil

¼ tsp Mustard seeds (*rai*)

1 Green chili, slit lengthwise

8 Curry leaves (*kadhi patta*)

METHOD

• Pour oil to the depth of ½" in a wok (*kadhai*) and heat until moderately hot. Deep-fry the okra pieces in hot oil until light golden brown; remove and drain on a paper towel.

• Whisk the strained yogurt with the chilled milk until smooth and refrigerate. Just before serving, mix the yogurt with cilantro, green chili, and ginger pastes, fried okra pieces, mustard powder, and salt to taste. Transfer to a serving bowl.

• **For the tempering,** heat the oil in a tempering ladle for 30 seconds; add the mustard seeds and when they splutter, add the green chili and curry leaves; mix and pour over the yogurt immediately.

• Use only tender, fresh green okra. Avoid okra that is discolored or limp, as this will alter the texture and taste of the dish.

• Mix the deep-fried okra with the yogurt mixture just before serving, to ensure that it remains crisp.

157 || ACCOMPANIMENTS || Pure & Special

CHILI PICKLE IN MINUTES
Chatpat Achaari Mirch

INGREDIENTS
¼ lb / 100 g Plump green chilies, washed, dried on paper towel, cut into 1" pieces
1 tsp / 5 g Coriander (*dhaniya*) powder
2 tsp / 10 g Fennel (*saunf*) powder
½ tsp / 2½ g Dried mango (*amchur*) powder
⅛ tsp Red chili powder
1 tsp / 5 g *Chaat masala* (see p. 214)
Salt to taste

For the seasoning:
1 tbsp / 15 ml Mustard oil (*sarson ka tel*)
A pinch Asafoetida (*hing*)
¼ tsp Fenugreek (*methi*) seeds
¼ tsp Cumin (*jeera*) seeds
⅛ tsp Turmeric (*haldi*) powder
2 tsp / 10 g Gram flour (*besan*)

METHOD
- Heat 1 tbsp mustard oil in a wok (*kadhai*) for 30 seconds; add the asafoetida, fenugreek seeds, cumin seeds, turmeric powder, and gram flour; cook on low heat for 10 seconds, stirring continuously. Add the green chili pieces and mix.

- Add the coriander, fennel, dried mango and red chili powders, *chaat masala,* and salt to taste.

- Mix and sauté on high heat for a minute, stirring continuously.

- Remove and serve.

> THE TOASTY FLAVOR OF GRAM FLOUR IN THIS PUNGENT, EASY-TO-PREPARE CHILI PICKLE ADDS A ZING TO ANY MEAL.

- Mustard oil is an ideal choice for pickles because of its smoky, pungent flavor and natural preservative properties.
- Plump, full chilies are recommended for this recipe.
- This pickle is often served along with Masala Maize Puffs (see p. 150).

TANGY ROOT RELISH
Achaari Kandmool

INGREDIENTS

1 lb / 500 g Turnips (*shalgam*), washed, peeled, cut into 1¼" long and ½" thick pieces
1 lb / 500 g Radishes (*mooli*), washed, peeled, cut into ½" discs
1 tsp / 5 g Red chili powder
1 tbsp / 15 g Salt
2 leveled tbsp / 20 g Mustard (*sarson*) powder
¼ tsp Asafoetida (*hing*)
1 tsp / 5 g Turmeric (*haldi*) powder
¼ cup / 50 ml Mustard oil (*sarson ka tel*)

METHOD

• Boil 3¾ cups water in a broad vessel, add the turnip and radish pieces, and bring to a boil on high heat. Drain in a colander and dry the pieces on a paper towel.

• Sun-dry the radish and turnip pieces for 2 hours or air dry them under a fan for 4 hours or until dry.

• On a large plate, mix the radish and turnip pieces with red chili powder, salt, mustard powder, asafoetida, turmeric powder, and mustard oil.

• Transfer to a bowl, cover, and set aside for two days, mixing occasionally. Transfer to a sterilized pickle jar. This pickle can be left at room temperature for 2 days, after which it needs to be stored in a refrigerator.

THIS PICKLE IS A WINTER DELICACY, FAVORED FOR ITS SHARP AND PUNGENT FLAVORS, AND CAN BE ENJOYED WITH ANY INDIAN MEAL.

• Mustard oil is easily available in Indian supermarkets.
• It is necessary to store mustard-based pickles in a refrigerator to prevent them from souring too much.

• In north India, this pickle is particularly enjoyed with Fenugreek Maize Bread (see p. 144) and Stuffed Millet Bread (see p. 148).

NUTTY SAFFRON MILK
Kesar Pista Doodh

Serves: 1

SERVED DURING WEDDINGS AND OTHER CELEBRATIONS IN NORTH INDIA, THIS AROMATIC DRINK IS ALSO A WELCOME BEVERAGE ON A CHILLY WINTER NIGHT.

INGREDIENTS
1¼ cups / 250 ml Milk
½-1 tsp / 2½-5 g Sugar
¼ tsp Saffron-green cardamom (*kesar-elaichi*) powder (see p. 219)
2 tsp / 7 g Almonds (*badam*), peeled, slivered (see p. 218)
1 tsp / 5 g Pistachios (*pista*), peeled, slivered (see p. 218)

METHOD
- Place the milk in a pan with sugar, saffron-green cardamom powder, 1 tsp almonds, and ½ tsp pistachios.

- Bring the mixture to a boil on moderate heat, stirring frequently; simmer for 8 minutes.

- Serve hot, sprinkled with remaining slivered almonds and pistachios.

- The quantities of sugar, almonds, and pistachios may be modified to your individual taste.

- If making larger quantities, increase the simmering time proportionately.

TANGY DUMPLING APÉRITIF
Pakodi Ki Kanji

IN NORTH INDIA, THIS DELICACY, WITH ITS UNUSUAL TANGY FLAVOR, IS MADE DURING THE FESTIVAL OF HOLI AND EATEN AS A PRELUDE TO THE MAIN MEAL TO PIQUE ONE'S APPETITE.

INGREDIENTS

¾ cup / 125 g Split skinned green gram lentils (*dhuli moong dal*), washed, soaked in plenty of water for 3 hours, drained
2 tsp / 10 g Chopped ginger (*adrak*)
2 tsp / 10 g Chopped green chilies
2 tsp / 10 g Fennel (*saunf*) seeds
Refined vegetable oil for deep-frying
2 slightly-heaped tbsp / 30 g Mustard (*sarson*) powder
1 tsp / 5 g Red chili powder
¼ tsp Asafoetida (*hing*)
Salt to taste

METHOD

* Grind the soaked green gram with ginger and green chilies to a thick batter in a blender / food processor, using very little water. Transfer the batter to a large bowl and whisk with an electric beater until light and fluffy. Test the batter by dropping ¼ tsp of the batter in about ½ cup water. If the batter floats, it is of the right consistency for soft dumplings.

* Add the fennel seeds to the batter and mix.

* Pour oil to the depth of 1" in a wok (*kadhai*) and heat until hot. With your fingers, drop small portions of the batter, in batches, into the hot oil and deep-fry the dumplings until light golden brown. Remove with a slotted spoon and drain on a paper towel.

* In a large bowl, mix 10 cups / 2¼ l water with the mustard powder, red chili powder, asafoetida, and salt to taste.

* Immerse the dumplings in this mustard water. Cover and set the bowl aside for 2 days, gently mixing occasionally.

* Serve on the third day and refrigerate any leftovers. Consume within two days.

* If the deep-fried dumplings have absorbed too much oil, plunge them into a large bowl of water for 20 seconds, remove, and then add to the mustard water.

SAFFRON KAHWAH
Kesari Kahwah

SERVED DURING FESTIVE MEALS IN SPECIALLY DESIGNED HANDLELESS-CUPS, THIS HOT KASHMIRI DRINK IS ENJOYED FOR ITS SUBTLE SAFFRON-CINNAMON FLAVOR.

INGREDIENTS

4 Green cardamom pods
(*choti elaichi*)
½" Cinnamon (*dalchini*) stick
A few strands Saffron (*kesar*)
Sugar to taste
To garnish:
6 Almonds (*badam*), peeled,
slivered (see p. 218)
A few strands Saffron, optional

METHOD

- Pour 2½ cups / 600 ml water into a pan, add the green cardamom pods and cinnamon stick and bring to a boil on moderate heat; simmer for 5 minutes.

- Add the saffron strands and sugar to taste and simmer the *kahwah* for 20 seconds. Sieve through a strainer.

- **To serve,** place 2 tsp slivered almonds in a cup and pour in the hot *kahwah* (or serve on the side, as pictured).

- Garnish with one or two strands of saffron and serve immediately.

- *Kahwah* can also be sweetened with honey, lending an unusual taste to its delicate flavor.

MINT TEA
Pudina Chai

INGREDIENTS
½-1 tsp / 2½-5 g Green
tea leaves
½ cup Mint (*pudina*) leaves
Honey (*shehed*) or sugar
to taste

METHOD
- Pour 4¼ cups / 1 l water into a pan or kettle and bring to a boil. Rinse a teapot with ½ cup boiling water and discard. Pour the green tea leaves into the teapot.

- Pour in the remaining boiling water. Place the lid on the teapot and brew, covered with a tea cosy, for 30 seconds to a minute (see tip).

- **To serve**, place 4-5 mint leaves in each teacup and pour in the brewed tea.

- Serve immediately with honey or sugar on the side.

REFRESHING
AND THERAPEUTIC,
THIS SUBTLY FLAVORED
MINT TEA CAN BE ENJOYED
AT ANY TIME OF THE DAY,
WHATEVER YOUR MOOD.

- You may need to alter the quantity of green tea and the brewing time, depending on the strength of the green tea you are using.

- Rinsing the teapot with boiling water ensures that the tea brews to perfection.

TANGY-SWEET SAUCE
Tikhi-Meethi Chutney

INGREDIENTS

3 tbsp / 45 ml White vinegar
(*safed sirka*)
2 tbsp / 30 g Sugar
¼ tsp Salt
¹/₈ tsp Red chili flakes

METHOD

- Mix the white vinegar, sugar, and salt in a pan and bring to a boil on low heat, stirring until the sugar dissolves.

- Continue to cook for a minute on low heat and set aside to cool.

- Mix in the chili flakes and serve. Refrigerate any leftovers.

- This sauce is used in Tangy Lettuce Wrap (see p. 38), Lotus Stem and Pasta Salad (see p. 40), Green Floret Fritters (see p. 72), and Lotus Stem Sandwich Fritters (see p. 74).

SWEET 'N' SOUR CHUTNEY
Khatti-Meethi Chutney

Makes ⅓ cup (80 ml)

INGREDIENTS
2 tbsp / 30 g Sugar
2 tsp / 10 g Dried mango
powder (*amchur*)
¼ tsp Salt
¼ tsp Red chili powder
¼ tsp *Garam masala* powder
(see p. 214)

METHOD
- In a pan, combine the sugar, dried mango powder, ½ cup / 100 ml water, and salt.

- Bring the mixture to a boil on low heat, stirring occasionally. Simmer for 10 minutes and set aside to cool.

- Add the red chili and *garam masala* powders; mix and serve. Refrigerate any leftovers.

- This chutney is used in Tangy Lettuce Wrap (see p. 38), Pasta Mélange (see p. 48), and Indian Burger (see p. 62).

CHILI GARLIC CHUTNEY
Lal Lehsuni Chutney

Makes ¾ cup (180 ml)

INGREDIENTS

30 Dried red chilies (*sookhi lal mirch*)
4 Garlic (*lasan*) cloves
1½ tsp / 7½ g Sugar
2 leveled tsp / 10 g Salt
⅓ cup / 70 ml (approx) White vinegar (*safed sirka*)
2 tsp / 10 ml Dark soy sauce

METHOD

• Mix the dried red chilies, garlic cloves, sugar, and salt with half the amount of white vinegar and grind to a smooth paste in a blender / food processor.

• Transfer to a serving bowl.

• Mix in the remaining white vinegar and soy sauce.

• Let the sauce stand, covered for 8 hours so that it matures to the ideal bite and pungency. If you need to dilute the sauce, use additional white vinegar. Do not use water, as it will spoil the sauce. Store at room temperature.

• If possible, use dried red Kashmiri chilies with a crinkly surface to ensure the perfect pungency.

• This chutney is used in Chilled Macbean Delight (see p. 44), Pasta Mélange (see p. 48), and Stuffed Mushroom Caps (see p. 78).

SPICY TOMATO CHUTNEY
Tikhi Tamatar Chutney

INGREDIENTS

1 tbsp / 15 ml Refined vegetable oil

½ tsp / 2½ g Finely-chopped garlic (*lasan*)

½ tsp / 2½ g Finely-chopped ginger (*adrak*)

½ tsp / 2½ g Finely-chopped green chilies

¹/₈ tsp Red chili powder

2 medium / 150 g Tomatoes, roasted, peeled (see p. 212), chopped into medium cubes

¼ tsp Sugar

¼ tsp Mint (*pudina*) paste (see p. 207)

1 Green cardamom (*choti elaichi*), seeds only, ground (see p. 219)

Salt to taste

METHOD

• Heat 1 tbsp oil in a pan for 30 seconds; add the garlic, ginger, green chilies, and red chili powder; mix.

• Lower the heat and add the tomatoes, sugar, mint paste, green cardamom seeds, and salt to taste. Add ¼ cup / 50 ml water and bring the mixture to a boil on moderate heat.

• Gently mash and simmer for 2 minutes, stirring occasionally. Cool and serve. Refrigerate any leftovers and consume within 2 days.

• This chutney is served with Lotus Pearl Kebabs (see p. 76).

YOGURT MUSTARD DIP
Dahi-Rai Chutney

INGREDIENTS

¾ cup / 150 g Yogurt (*dahi*)
1 tsp / 5 g Mustard (*sarson*) or
mustard powder
¼ tsp Red chili flakes
Salt to taste

METHOD

• Strain the yogurt in a fine
 sieve for 20 minutes; discard
 the whey and whisk the
 strained yogurt; refrigerate.

• Mix the whisked yogurt with
 mustard, red chili flakes, and
 salt to taste.

• Serve chilled and refrigerate
 any leftovers. Consume within
 2 days.

• This dip is served with Hint 'o' Mint Cheese Tikka (see p. 66).

DATE YOGURT DIP
Khajoori Dahi Chutney

INGREDIENTS
½ cup / 100 g Yogurt (*dahi*)
1 tbsp / 15 g Finely-chopped,
semi-soft dates (*khajoor*)
A pinch Red chili flakes
2 Mint (*pudina*) leaves, crushed
with a mortar and pestle
Salt to taste

METHOD
• Place the yogurt in a fine sieve for half an hour; discard the whey
and whisk the strained yogurt, refrigerate.

• Just before serving, mix the whisked yogurt with dates, red chili
flakes, crushed mint leaves, and salt to taste.

• Refrigerate any leftovers and consume within 2 days.

• This dip is served alongside Broccoli Cheese Kebabs (see p. 70).

GARLIC GREEN CHUTNEY
Lehsuni Hari Chutney

INGREDIENTS

1 (loosely-packed) cup Cilantro (*dhaniya*) leaves
1 (loosely-packed) cup Mint (*pudina*) leaves
3 tsp / 15 g Chopped green chilies
1 tsp / 5 g Chopped garlic (*lasan*)
½ tsp / 2½ g Yogurt (*dahi*)
Salt to taste
1-2 tsp / 5-10 ml Lemon juice (*nimbu ka ras*)

METHOD

• In a blender / food processor, purée the cilantro and mint leaves, green chilies, garlic, yogurt, and salt to taste to a smooth paste, using very little water, if necessary; refrigerate.

• Transfer to a serving bowl.

• Just before serving, add the lemon juice to taste and mix. Refrigerate any leftovers and consume within two days.

• To ensure this chutney retains its green color, add the lemon juice just before serving.

GREEN COCONUT CHUTNEY
Hari Nariyal Chutney

INGREDIENTS

1 (tightly-packed) cup Cilantro (*dhaniya*) leaves

¼ (loosely-packed) cup Mint (*pudina*) leaves

1 tbsp / 15 g Grated fresh coconut (*nariyal*; see p. 210)

2 heaped tsp / 10 g Peanuts (*moongphalli*), skinned (see p. 215)

1 tsp / 5 g Yogurt (*dahi*)

2 tsp / 10 g Chopped green chilies

Salt to taste

1-2 tsp / 5-10 ml Lemon juice (*nimbu ka ras*)

METHOD

- In a blender / food processor, purée the cilantro and mint leaves, coconut, peanuts, yogurt, green chilies, and salt to taste to a fine paste, adding very little water, if necessary; refrigerate.

- Transfer to a serving bowl.

- Just before serving, add the lemon juice and mix. Refrigerate any leftovers and consume within a day.

- This chutney is served alongside Spicy Sweet Corn Patties (see p. 55) and Spicy Gram Flour Rolls (see p. 60).

MINT YOGURT CHUTNEY
Pudina Dahi Chutney

INGREDIENTS

¾ cup / 150 g Yogurt (*dahi*)
1 (tightly-packed) cup Mint (*pudina*) leaves
1 tsp / 5 g Chopped green chilies
1 tsp / 5 g Chopped fresh ginger (*adrak*)
1 tbsp / 4 g Chopped cilantro (*dhaniya*) leaves
Salt to taste
1 tsp / 5 ml Lemon juice (*nimbu ka ras*)

METHOD

- Pour the yogurt into a sieve and drain for 20 minutes; discard the whey and whisk the strained yogurt; refrigerate.

- In a blender / food processor, purée the mint leaves, green chilies, ginger, and cilantro leaves with salt to taste until smooth, using very little water, if necessary.

- Transfer to a serving bowl and refrigerate.

- Just before serving, mix the mint chutney with the whisked yogurt, lemon juice, and salt (if required) and serve immediately. Keep any leftovers refrigerated and consume within a day.

- This chutney is used in Kebab 'o' Lentil (see p. 58) and Cheese Tikka à la Saffron (see p. 68).

PICKLED ONIONS
Pyaz Sirkewale

Makes ¾ cup (185 g)

INGREDIENTS
2 medium / 150 g Onions,
cut into thin slices
2 tbsp / 30 ml White vinegar
(*safed sirka*)
½ tsp / 2½ g *Chaat masala*
(see p. 214)
1 tsp / 1 g Finely-chopped
cilantro (*dhaniya*) leaves
Salt to taste

METHOD
• Mix the onion slices with
white vinegar, *chaat masala*,
cilantro, and salt to taste.

• Toss in a mixing bowl; serve.

• Keep any leftovers
refrigerated and consume
within a day.

• This dish is served as an accompaniment to Kebab 'o' Lentil (see p. 58)
and Cheese Tikka à la Saffron (see p. 68).

COCONUT CHUTNEY
Nariyal Chutney

INGREDIENTS

1 cup / 50 g Grated fresh
coconut (*nariyal*; see p. 210)
¼ cup / 35 g Peanuts
(*moongphalli*), skinned (see p. 215)
2 Dried red chilies (*sookhi
lal mirch*)
1 tbsp / 4 g Chopped cilantro
(*dhaniya*) leaves
1 tsp / 5 g Chopped fresh
ginger (*adrak*)
Salt to taste

For the tempering:

2 tsp / 10 ml Refined
vegetable oil
¼ tsp Mustard seeds (*rai*)
8 Curry leaves (*kadhi patta*)

METHOD

- In a blender / food processor, grind the coconut, peanuts, chilies, cilantro leaves, ginger, salt to taste, and ½–¾ cup / 100–150 ml water to a smooth paste. Transfer to a serving bowl.

- **For the tempering,** heat 2 tsp oil in a tempering ladle for 20 seconds; add the mustard seeds; when they splutter, add the curry leaves and immediately pour onto the purée and serve.

- Refrigerate any leftovers and consume within a day.

- This chutney is served with Stuffed Lentil Pancakes (see p. 56).

PEANUT CHUTNEY
Moongphalli Chutney

INGREDIENTS

6 tbsp / 90 ml Refined vegetable oil (4 tbsp + 2 tbsp)
2 tbsp / 20 g Peanuts (*moongphalli*)
¼ tsp Red chili powder
1½ tsp / 7½ g Sugar
¼ tsp Salt
¼ tsp Cornstarch
2 tbsp / 30 ml White vinegar (*safed sirka*)

METHOD

- Heat 4 tbsp oil in a tempering ladle or a small frying pan for a minute. Add the peanuts and fry on low heat until evenly dark brown, taking care not to burn them; remove and cool.

- In a blender / food processor, combine the fried peanuts with red chili powder, sugar, salt, and 2 tbsp oil and grind to a fine paste; set aside.

- In a bowl, combine cornstarch with ½ cup / 100 ml water and mix until smooth.

- In a pan, combine the ground peanut paste, white vinegar, and cornstarch paste. Bring the mixture to a boil on moderate heat, stirring constantly.

- Cool and serve. Refrigerate any leftovers and use within a week.

- This chutney is used in Tangy Lettuce Wrap (see p. 38), Nutty Paneer (see p. 65), and Green Floret Fritters (see p. 72).

DESSERTS

CREAMY FRUIT 'N' NUT DELIGHT
Angoori Rabadi

INGREDIENTS

7½ cups / 1¾ l Milk
3 leveled tbsp / 45 g Sugar
2 Green cardamom pods (*choti elaichi*), seeds only, ground (see p. 219)
1 tsp / 5 ml Rose water (*gulab jal*)
½ cup / 75 g Pomegranate seeds (*anar ke dane*), fresh
½ cup / 75 g Seedless green grapes (*angoor*)
1 tbsp / 10 g Almonds (*badam*), peeled (see p. 218)
1 tbsp / 10 g Pistachios (*pista*), peeled (see p. 218)

METHOD

• Pour the milk in a heavy-bottomed wok (*kadhai*) and bring to a boil on high heat, stirring frequently. Lower the heat and cook until the milk reduces to a quarter of its original volume, stirring occasionally.

• Add the sugar and bring the mixture to a boil on moderate heat; simmer for 2 minutes and turn off the heat. Add the ground cardamom seeds, mix, and set aside to cool.

• Add the rose water, mix, and refrigerate the mixture (*rabadi*).

• Just before serving, gently mix the fresh and dried fruits and nuts with the chilled *rabadi*, reserving some for the garnish, and transfer to a serving dish or into individual serving bowls.

• Serve garnished with reserved fruits and nuts.

THIS PUDDING HAS AN INTERESTING GRANULAR TEXTURE THAT COMBINES PERFECTLY WITH THE NATURAL SWEETNESS OF FRESH FRUIT.

• The traditional version of this recipe uses mango as the main fruit. Whatever fruits you use, add them just before serving, as they tend to release water and will dilute the *rabadi*.

• This *rabadi* is delicious enough to be prepared only with nuts.

• Rose water is made by distilling fresh rose petals. Its subtle flavor and fragrance is used to enhance some Indian desserts.

SAFFRON FOX NUT PUDDING
Kesari Makhana Kheer

INGREDIENTS
2 oz / 50 g Fox nuts (*makhana*)
¼ tsp Saffron (*kesar*)
4 Green cardamom pods (*choti elaichi*), seeds only
4¼ cups / 1 l Milk
1½-2 tbsp / 25-30 g Sugar

To garnish:
2 tbsp / 20 g Almonds (*badam*), peeled (see p. 218)
1 tbsp / 10 g Pistachios (*pista*), peeled (see p. 218)

METHOD
• Remove the hard, black outer shells of the fox nuts.

• Cut each fox nut into four pieces; set aside.

• Pound the saffron and green cardamom seeds to a fine powder in a mortar and pestle (see p. 219).

• In a heavy-bottomed wok (*kadhai*), bring the milk to a boil on high heat, stirring often.

• Wash the fox nut pieces with plenty of water; squeeze by hand to remove any excess water and add to the boiling milk.

• Bring the mixture to a boil and continue cooking on low heat until the milk is reduced to a third of its original volume, stirring occasionally. Add the sugar, stir, and bring the mixture to a boil again on high heat; lower the heat and simmer for 10 minutes.

• Add the cardamom-saffron powder and mix. Turn off the heat and set aside to cool.

• Refrigerate and serve chilled, garnished with peeled almonds and pistachios. Consume within two days.

• Fox nuts (*makhana*) are also known as gorgon nuts. Often mistaken for lotus pods, they actually belong to the water lily family. They are easily available in Indian grocery stores.

THIS NON-CEREAL
DESSERT IS OFTEN SERVED
DURING FASTING RITUALS
IN NORTHERN
INDIA.

• Discard any hard fox nuts (not puffed up) that may have made it into the package.

DATE PINEAPPLE SURPRISE
Lajawaab Khajoori Ananas

INGREDIENTS

2 tbsp / 30 g Clarified butter
(ghee)
2 tbsp / 20 g Almonds (badam)
2 tbsp / 25 g Cashew
nuts (kaju)
4 / 275 g Pineapple (ananas)
slices, ¾" thick, cut into 4 pieces,
discarding hard center portion
3½ tbsp / 55 g Sugar
¼ tsp Lemon (nimbu) zest
(see tip)
2 oz / 50 g Whole milk fudge
(khoya, see p. 203), grated
2 tbsp Soft dates (khajoor),
cut into strips
A pinch Cinnamon (dalchini)
powder
A pinch Red chili flakes

METHOD

- In a small pan or wok (kadhai), heat 1 tbsp clarified butter for 30 seconds and fry the almonds on low heat until light golden brown; set aside. In the same pan, fry the cashew nuts on low heat until light golden brown; set aside.

- In a flat pan, heat ½ tbsp clarified butter for 30 seconds; add half the pineapple wedges and lightly caremelize on both sides over moderate heat; remove and cool. Add ½ tbsp clarified butter to the pan and repeat the process with the remaining pineapple wedges.

- Now cut the cooled pineapple wedges into 1" pieces and set aside.

- In a pan, heat the sugar with 1 tbsp / 15 ml water; cook on moderate heat until the sugar dissolves, stirring continuously.

- Add the lemon rind and pineapple pieces; cook for a minute on moderate heat, stirring gently.

- Add the grated whole milk fudge and continue to cook for a minute, stirring gently.

- Add the date strips, cinnamon powder, and red chili flakes.

- Add the fried almonds and cashew nuts; mix and serve immediately.

- Using a grater or zester, finely grate the outer peel of a whole, unwaxed lemon.

THE COMBINATION OF FRUIT, NUTS, WHOLE MILK FUDGE, AND A HINT OF CHILI, GIVES THIS DESSERT A DISTINCTIVE TEXTURE AND FLAVOR.

• This warming dessert tastes best when freshly prepared and cannot be made in advance.

SESAME MILK FUDGE TEMPTATION
Til Khoya Bahaar

INGREDIENTS

2 cups / 250 g White sesame (*safed til*) seeds

1 lb / 500 g Whole milk fudge (*khoya*; see p. 203)

1¾ cups / 250 g Powdered sugar (see p. 217)

8 Green cardamom pods (*choti elaichi*), seeds only, ground (see p. 219)

1½ tbsp / 15 g Pistachios (*pista*), slivered (see p. 218)

METHOD

- Pour the sesame seeds through a sieve. Heat a wok (*kadhai*) and toast the seeds on low heat, until evenly light golden brown, stirring occasionally. While still hot, grind coarsely in a blender / food processor.

- Place the whole milk fudge in a wok (*kadhai*) and fry on moderate heat, stirring continuously until the fudge pulls away from the sides of the wok and you can see melted clarified butter.

- Immediately combine the hot whole milk fudge with the warm, ground sesame seeds.

- Add the powdered sugar and green cardamom powder.

- Mix and knead well by hand.

- While the mixture is still hot, pull off small portions with your fingers and press, shaping into smooth, round balls.

- In case the mixture cools, sprinkle it with a little milk and continue.

- Using the slim handle of a teaspoon, make a slight depression on top of each ball and press a few pistachio slivers into the indent.

- Cool and serve. Consume within a week.

- Toasting the sesame seeds enhances their nutty flavor.

- 1¼ cups of granulated sugar will make 1¾ cups of powdered sugar.

Makes: 25-30 pieces

ALSO KNOWN AS *TIL LADOO*, THIS CRUNCHY SESAME DESSERT IS SERVED DURING THE INDIAN HARVEST FESTIVALS OF SANKRANTI AND LOHRI.

• Shape the mixture into small balls while hot, as it tends to harden as it cools.

• Ready-made whole milk fudge can be found in Indian grocery stores.

SWEET CRESCENTS ROYALE
Shahi Gunjia

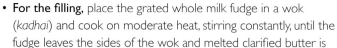

INGREDIENTS

For the filling:
½ lb / 250 g Whole milk fudge
(*khoya*), grated (see p. 203)
⅓ cup / 50 g Semolina (*sooji*)
1 cup / 150 g Powdered sugar
(see p. 217)
10 Green cardamom pods
(*choti elaichi*), seeds only, ground
(see p. 219)
4 tbsp / 40 g Almonds (*badam*),
slivered (see p. 218)
2 tbsp / 30 g Raisins (*kishmish*),
chopped
1 tbsp / 10 g Pistachios (*pista*),
slivered, to garnish

For the dough:
2 cups / 250 g All-purpose flour
3½ tbsp / 50 ml Melted
clarified butter
Lukewarm water to make
the dough

To seal the crecents:
2 tsp / 10 g All-purpose flour
(*maida*)

For deep-frying:
2 cups / 400 g Clarified butter

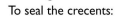

METHOD

- **For the filling,** place the grated whole milk fudge in a wok (*kadhai*) and cook on moderate heat, stirring constantly, until the fudge leaves the sides of the wok and melted clarified butter is seen; remove and cool.

- Heat a separate wok (*kadhai*); add the semolina and toast on low heat, stirring occasionally, until evenly light golden brown; remove and cool.

- Mix together the cooled semolina and whole milk fudge with powdered sugar, powdered green cardamom seeds, almonds, and raisins; set aside.

- **For the dough,** sieve the all-purpose flour; add melted clarified butter and gently knead into a flaky, semi-hard dough with lukewarm water. Cover with a moist cloth and let it stand for 15 minutes.

- **To make the crescents** (*gunjia*), mix 2 tsp all-purpose flour with a little water to make a semi-thick, smooth paste to seal the pastries.

- Divide the dough into equal balls and roll into thin 3½" discs.

- Apply the sealing paste lightly around the edge of each disc and place 1½ tsp of the filling in the center.

- Fold into a crescent. Press the edges to seal.

- Crimp gently with your thumb and index finger to create a frill.

- Set aside, covered in a moist cloth, while preparing the remaining crescents.

- Heat 2 cups clarified butter in a wok (*kadhai*) and deep-fry the crescents in batches of 6-8 on moderate heat, until light golden brown.

- Remove with a slotted spoon and transfer to a sieve. Cool and serve, garnished with slivered pistachios.

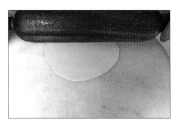

- Cooling the toasted semolina and whole milk fudge before mixing with the powdered sugar prevents a lumpy filling.

- The crimp design is traditionally done by hand, however, crescent molds can also be used.

GUNJIAS ARE SERVED DURING THE INDIAN FESTIVALS OF HOLI AND DIWALI AND ARE DELICIOUS ENOUGH TO BE PART OF THE *NAIVEDYA* (FOOD OFFERED TO THE LORD). OFTEN, IN LARGE FAMILIES, IT IS TRADITIONAL FOR THE WOMEN TO GATHER TOGETHER TO PREPARE THIS SWEETMEAT.

• Placing the crescents in a sieve after frying prevents them from becoming moist and soggy.

• Leftover filling can be used to prepare sweet, stuffed Indian bread, known as *mewa parathas*.

EXOTIC LENTIL PUDDING
Jashan-e-Moong Halwa

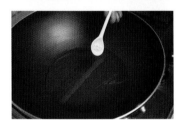

INGREDIENTS
¾ cup / 125 g Skinned split green gram lentils (*dhuli moong dal*), soaked in plenty of water for 2 hours, drained
10 Green cardamom pods (*choti elaichi*), seeds only
¼ tsp Saffron (*kesar*)
¾ cup / 150 g Sugar
½ cup / 125 g Clarified butter (*ghee*)
¼ tsp Whole-wheat flour (*atta*)
2½ oz / 75 g Whole milk fudge (*khoya*, see p. 203), grated
2 tbsp / 20 g Almonds (*badam*), peeled, slivered (see p. 218)
2 tbsp / 20 g Pistachios (*pista*), peeled, slivered (see p. 218)

METHOD
- Coarsely grind the green gram lentils in a blender / food processor until just short of fine in texture, using very little water, if required.
- Pound together the green cardamom seeds and saffron to a fine powder in a mortar and pestle and set aside (see p. 219).
- **For the sugar syrup,** mix the sugar with 1½ cups / 350 ml water in a pan and bring to a boil on low heat, stirring until the sugar dissolves; set aside.
- Heat ½ cup clarified butter in a nonstick wok (*kadhai*); add ¼ tsp whole-wheat flour (to prevent sticking).
- Add the ground green gram lentils and fry on low heat, stirring constantly.
- Use the back of the spoon to keep breaking and smoothing the lumps that form. Continue stirring until the mixture turns evenly granular and golden brown.
- Add the grated whole milk fudge, mix, and cook on low heat for 2 minutes, stirring constantly.
- Add the sugar syrup and cook on moderate heat, stirring constantly, until the mixture thickens.
- Sprinkle on 1 tbsp / 15 ml water, mix, and cook for 2 minutes, stirring constantly. Sprinkle on another tablespoon of water and continue to cook for another 2 minutes, stirring continuously.
- Add the green cardamom and saffron powder and 1½ tablespoons / 25 g clarified butter; mix gently. Serve hot, garnished with slivered almonds and pistachios.

- Sprinkling 2 tbsp water over the pudding while cooking gives it a fluffy, granular texture.

- Indian desserts taste best when made with clarified butter. Do not substitute it with butter or refined oil.

THE RICH
FLAVOR AND TEXTURE
OF THIS MAJESTIC INDIAN
DESSERT MAKES IT A FAVORITE
FOR CELEBRATIONS AND
FESTIVITIES.

• Preparing this dessert requires a fair amount of patience, but the delicious result is well worth the effort.

• This dessert can be stored in a refrigerator for up to two weeks.

NUTTY CALABASH DELIGHT
Lazeez Lauki Lachche

INGREDIENTS

1 lb / ½ kg Bottle gourd (*lauki*)
½ lb / 200 g Whole milk fudge (*khoya*, see p. 203)
½ cup / 100 g Sugar
8 Green cardamom pods (*choti elaichi*), seeds only, ground (see p. 219)
2 tbsp / 30 g Raw sugar crystals (*mishri*)
1 tsp / 5 ml Rose water (*gulab jal*)
3 tbsp / 30 g Almondettes (*chironji*; 2 tbsp + 1 tbsp)
2 tbsp / 20 g Almonds (*badam*), peeled, halved
1 tbsp / 10 g Pistachios (*pista*), peeled

For the lemon water, mix and set aside:
4¼ cups / 1 l Water
2 tsp / 10 ml Lemon juice (*nimbu ka ras*)

METHOD

• Peel and grate the bottle gourd and immediately immerse in the lemon water; let it stand for 5 minutes.

• Drain in a colander and pat dry with a paper towel; set aside.

• Place the whole milk fudge in a wok (*kadhai*) and fry on moderate heat, stirring continuously until the fudge leaves the sides of the wok and melted clarified butter is seen; set aside. When cool, break the whole milk fudge into small pieces by hand and set aside.

• In a wok (*kadhai*), combine the grated bottle gourd and sugar.

• Cook on moderate heat, stirring continuously, until the sugar evenly coats the bottle gourd or a thin layer of sugar appears on the surface of the wok.

• Add the crumbled whole milk fudge, powdered green cardamom seeds, raw sugar crystals, and rose water.

• Add 2 tbsp almondettes; mix and cook for a minute, stirring constantly. Set aside to cool.

• Serve at room temperature, garnished with almonds and pistachios and the remaining 1 tbsp of almondettes.

ENJOY THIS NUTTY DESSERT FOR ITS BLEND OF CRYSTALLINE SUGAR AND CRUNCHY ALMONDETTES, COMPLEMENTED BY THE DISTINCTIVE FLORAL UNDERTONES OF ROSE WATER.

• Immersing grated bottle gourd in lemon water prevents it from discoloring, and gives it a translucent sheen.

• Raw sugar crystals are coarse sugar granules that are three to four times larger than refined granulated sugar.

• Almondette is a tiny seed, also known as Cuddapah almond or charoli. It is commonly used in Indian desserts.

STRAWBERRY RICE PUDDING
Strawberry Phirni

INGREDIENTS

¹/₃ cup / 50 g Basmati rice, soaked in plenty of water for 2 hours, drained
4¼ cups / 1 l Milk (at room temperature)
1 tsp / 5 g Strawberry custard powder
1 tsp / 5 ml Strawberry essence
½ cup / 100 g Sugar
A few drops Red food coloring, optional

To garnish:
10 medium Strawberries, hulled and sliced
A few sprigs Mint (*pudina*) leaves

METHOD

• Grind the rice with very little water to a smooth paste in a blender / food processor. Sieve and set aside.

• Combine 2 tbsp milk with the strawberry custard powder and mix well until smooth.

• To the remaining milk, add the sieved rice and custard powder paste, whisking well to remove any lumps.

• Transfer to a wok (*kadhai*) and cook on moderate heat, stirring constantly until the mixture comes to a boil. Turn off the heat, add the strawberry essence, sugar, and the food coloring, if using; stir and then turn the heat back on.

• Continue cooking on moderate heat, stirring constantly, until bubbles begin to appear in the center of the mixture.

• Test the consistency by dropping ¼ tsp of the rice mixture into a small bowl of room-temperature water; if it forms a ball, it has cooked completely.

• Immediately turn off the heat and spoon the pudding into individual serving bowls or a flat 8"-diameter dish. Cool to room temperature; cover with plastic wrap, and refrigerate for 8 hours.

• Serve garnished with strawberry slices and mint leaves.

THIS FLAVORED RICE PUDDING IS TRADITIONALLY SERVED IN PETITE, EARTHENWARE POTS AND IS SAVORED FOR ITS SMOOTH TEXTURE COMPLEMENTED BY THE CRUNCH OF FRESH STRAWBERRIES.

• Always mix the rice paste into room-temperature milk, so that the pudding does not become lumpy.

• Keep the serving bowls or dish ready and spoon in the pudding while it is still hot. Do not delay this process—the pudding begins to set almost immediately.

  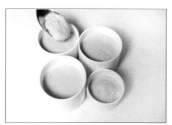 

• You can omit the red food coloring if you have any reservations.

CHEESY CAKE À LA CITRON
Khushnuma Cheesecake

INGREDIENTS

1 tsp / 5 g Butter (at room temperature), for greasing
1 leveled cup / 100 g All-purpose flour (*maida*)
1¼ tsp / 6¼ g Baking powder
¾ tsp / 3¾ g Baking soda
A pinch Salt
¼ tsp Lemon zest (see tip)
¾ cup / 200 g Condensed milk
4 tbsp / 60 g Cold unsalted butter
¾ cup / 150 ml Milk
1 tsp / 5 ml Lemon juice (*nimbu ka ras*)
2 oz / 60 g Cheese, grated

A FLUFFY CAKE WITH A SUBTLE LEMON TANG, THIS DELECTABLE DESSERT CAN BE SERVED WITH FRESH WHIPPED CREAM, VANILLA ICE CREAM, OR CUSTARD WITH FRESH ORANGE CHUNKS.

METHOD

- Preheat the oven to 350°F / 180°C for about 10-15 minutes. Line a 7" round cake pan with parchment paper and grease with 1 tsp butter (see p. 217).

- Sift the flour, baking powder, baking soda, and salt; add the lemon zest and mix.

- Pour the condensed milk into a large mixing bowl. Cut the butter into cubes and add to the condensed milk. Using an electric mixer, beat until fluffy and creamy, moving the mixer in a clockwise motion.

- Add the milk, and with the electric mixer turned off, stir gently. Now add the lemon juice, grated cheese, and the flour mixture and combine well using the cut and fold method (see p. 217).

- Turn the electric mixer on and beat for 10 seconds, moving the mixer in a clockwise motion to ensure that all the ingredients combine completely.

- Transfer the cake batter to the prepared cake pan and gently even out the top with a spatula.

- Bake at 350°F / 180°C for 25-35 minutes or until done (to check, insert a toothpick in the center of the cake, if it comes out clean, the cake is ready).

- Remove the cake pan from the oven and cool for 10-15 minutes. Run a sharp knife along the inside of the pan to loosen the cake. Unmold carefully onto a wire rack (this prevents the base of the cake from becoming moist) and peel off the parchment paper.

- Transfer to a platter and serve warm.

- To obtain lemon zest, grate the outer skin of a fresh lemon using a zester or a sharp grater.

- As the condensed milk is sweet enough for this cake, sugar is not required.

• It is important to follow the cut and fold method (see p. 217) to mix the batter, as this technique helps incorporate air into the mixture, ensuring a light and fluffy cake.

GATEAU CHOCO-LAIT
Chai-Time Choco Cake

INGREDIENTS

1 tsp / 5 g Butter (at room temperature), for greasing
2 leveled cups / 200 g All-purpose flour (*maida*)
1¼ tsp / 6¼ g Baking powder
1 tsp / 5 g Baking soda
3 tbsp / 45 g Unsweetened cocoa powder
¼ tsp Salt
¾ cup / 200 g Condensed milk
7 tbsp / 100 g Cold unsalted butter
¾ cup / 150 ml Milk
1 cup / 150 g Powdered sugar (see p. 217)
½ cup / 100 g Yogurt (*dahi*)
1 tbsp / 15 ml Dark rum
1 tsp / 5 ml Vanilla essence
7 oz / 200 g Walnut (*akhrot*) halves, to garnish

For the chocolate glaze icing:
1½ tbsp / 45 g Butter
2 tbsp / 30 g Unsweetened cocoa powder
3 slightly-heaped tbsp / 45 g Confectioner's sugar

THIS DELICIOUS CAKE, CROWNED WITH A SHINY CHOCOLATE GLAZE AND DECORATED WITH CRUNCHY WALNUT HALVES IS HEAVEN FOR CHOCOLATE LOVERS.

METHOD

- Preheat the oven to 350°F / 180°C for about 10-15 minutes. Line a 9" round cake pan with parchment paper and grease with 1 tsp butter (see p. 217).

- Sieve the all-purpose flour with baking powder, baking soda, unsweetened cocoa powder, and salt; set aside.

- Pour the condensed milk into a large mixing bowl. Cut the butter into cubes and add to the condensed milk. Using an electric mixer, beat until fluffy and creamy, moving the mixer in a clockwise motion.

- Add the milk, and with the electric mixer turned off, stir gently. Add the powdered sugar, yogurt, rum, vanilla essence, 2 tbsp / 30 ml water, and the all-purpose flour mixture and mix well using the cut and fold method (see p. 217).

- Turn the electric mixer on and beat for 10 seconds, moving the mixer in a clockwise motion to ensure that all the ingredients are completely mixed.

- Transfer the cake batter to the prepared cake pan and gently even out the top with a spatula. Bake at 350°F / 180°C for 40-60 minutes or until done (to check, insert a toothpick in the center of the cake; if it comes out clean, the cake is ready).

- Remove the cake pan from the oven and cool for 10-15 minutes. Run a sharp knife along the inside of the pan to loosen the cake. Unmold carefully onto a wire rack (this prevents the base of the cake from becoming moist) and peel off the parchment paper. When the cake is completely cool, place it upside down on a platter.

- **For the icing,** place the butter, unsweetened cocoa powder, confectioner's sugar, and 1 tbsp / 15 ml water in pan. Cook on low heat, stirring constantly until it comes to a boil. Turn off the heat.

- Wait until the cake is completely cool to pour the hot icing over it. This will prevent the cake from becoming soggy.

- Immediately pour the icing over the cake. Use the underside of a spoon to spread the icing evenly.

- Decorate with walnut halves, let stand for one hour, and serve.

- If the cake has risen to a dome shape in the center, level by trimming the top with a sharp knife, before turning upside-down and icing.

GOLDEN CINNAPPLE CAKE
Sunhera Apple Cake

INGREDIENTS

1 tsp / 5 g Butter (at room temperature), for greasing
1 cup / 125 g All-purpose flour (*maida*)
1¼ tsp / 6¼ g Baking powder
½ tsp / 2½ g Baking soda
A pinch Salt
¾ cup / 200 g Condensed milk
4 tbsp / 60 g Cold unsalted butter, cut into cubes
¾ cup / 150 ml Milk
1 tsp / 5 ml Vanilla essence
2 tbsp / 30 ml Heavy cream

For the topping:

2 medium / 250 g Apples (*seb*)
2 tsp / 10 ml Lemon juice (*nimbu ka ras*)
2 tbsp / 20 g Walnuts (*akhrot*), chopped
2 tbsp / 30 g Raisins (*kishmish*), chopped
1 tsp / 5 g Cinnamon (*dalchini*) powder

METHOD

• Preheat the oven to 350°F / 180°C for about 10-15 minutes. Line a 7" round cake pan with parchment paper and grease with 1 tsp butter (see p. 217).

• Peel, core, and slice the apples. Evenly coat the slices with 2 tsp lemon juice to prevent browning; set aside.

• Sift the all-purpose flour with baking powder, baking soda, and salt; set aside.

• Pour the condensed milk into a large mixing bowl. Add the butter, and, using an electric mixer, beat until fluffy and creamy, moving the mixer in a clockwise motion. Add the milk, and with the electric mixer turned off, stir gently.

• Now add the vanilla essence, cream, and the flour mixture; combine well using the cut and fold method (see p. 217). Turn the electric mixer on and beat for 10 seconds, moving it in a clockwise motion to ensure that all the ingredients combine completely.

• Transfer the cake batter to the prepared cake pan and gently even out the top with a spatula.

• Arrange the apple slices in concentric circles on top and sprinkle in the chopped walnuts, raisins, and cinnamon powder.

• Bake at 350°F / 180°C for 30-40 minutes or until done (to check, insert a toothpick in the center of the cake; if it comes out clean, the cake is ready). Remove the cake pan from the oven and cool for 10-15 minutes. Run a sharp knife along the inside of the pan to loosen the cake. Carefully unmold onto a wire rack (this prevents the base of the cake from becoming moist) and peel off the parchment paper.

• Transfer to a platter and serve warm.

THE SIGNATURE APPLE-CINNAMON PAIRING COMES ALIVE IN THIS DELICIOUS AND SIMPLE EGGLESS CAKE, BEST SERVED WARM, ACCOMPANIED WITH VANILLA ICE CREAM OR A CUP OF COFFEE.

• Preheating the oven until it reaches the required baking temperature (usually for at least 10-15 minutes), ensures a light and fluffy cake.

• To make a basic, eggless vanilla cake, omit the topping ingredients.

COOKING PROCESSES

WORKING WITH DAIRY
YOGURT

HOMEMADE YOGURT

1
- Heat 4¼ cups / 1 l milk until lukewarm (40°-45°C).

2
- Place ½ tsp yogurt culture in a bowl.

3
- Pour in the lukewarm milk and mix well.

4
- Cover and keep in a warm, dry place for 3-6 hours or until it sets.

STRAINED OR HUNG YOGURT (*CHAKKA*)

- Place 2 cups / 400 g yogurt in a sieve and leave for 3-4 hours. Discard the whey and use as per the recipe.

YOGURT FOR RAITAS AND DIPS

1
- Place 2 cups / 400 g yogurt (or as per recipe) in a sieve for 20-30 minutes.

2
- Discard the whey.
- Whisk with ¼ cup / 50 ml chilled milk (or as per recipe) until smooth and creamy.

TIPS
YOGURT
- Do not use hot milk to set yogurt, as this will alter its taste and texture.
- Yogurt usually sets faster during summer, compared to winter.
- After setting, yogurt needs to be refrigerated to prevent souring.

WHOLE MILK FUDGE (*KHOYA*)

- Place 4¼ cups / 1 l whole milk in a heavy-bottomed wok (*kadhai*).

- Cook on moderate heat until the milk reduces to a quarter of its original volume, stirring occasionally.

- Lower the heat and keep stirring (to prevent sticking) until it becomes semi-solid. Cool and refrigerate, covered.

TIPS
WHOLE MILK FUDGE
- 4¼ cups / 1 l of milk makes about 6 oz /175 g of whole milk fudge.
- After refrigeration, it must be consumed within 3-4 days.
- Packaged whole milk fudge can be found in Indian grocery stores.

PANEER

HOMEMADE PLAIN PANEER

- Bring 4¼ cups / 1 l milk to a boil in a pan, on moderate heat. Turn off the heat and add 1-2 tbsp lemon juice.

- Gradually stir until the milk curdles.
- Let it stand for 2 minutes.

- Drain in a cloth sieve / muslin cloth.

- Tie the ends of the cloth. Let it stand in a colander for 5 minutes for set cheese and 10 minutes to grate and mash.

GRATING AND MASHING

- After 10 minutes, unwrap. Hand-grate the cheese.

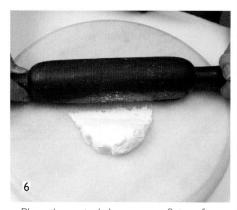

- Place the grated cheese on a flat surface and mash to a smooth paste with a rolling pin. Use as per the recipe or to make set paneer.

HOMEMADE SET PANEER

- After 5 minutes, fold the cloth over the cheese, molding into a square.

- Place a light weight over the square for 20 minutes.

- Gently unwrap the cheese. Place on a flat surface and cut off any uneven edges.

HOMEMADE MASALA PANEER

- Place 4¼ cups / 1 l milk in a pan. Add ¼ tsp salt, 1 tsp cumin seeds, 1 tsp finely-chopped green chilies, and 2 tbsp finely-chopped cilantro leaves and bring to a boil over moderate heat. Turn off the heat and add 1-2 tbsp lemon juice. Gradually stir until the milk curdles.

TIPS
PANEER

- 4¼ cups / 1 l of milk makes about ¼ lb / 125 g of paneer.
- **To obtain soft paneer,** turn the heat off immediately after the milk comes to a boil. After placing the paneer in a muslin cloth, do not squeeze. Allow to stand for 5 minutes or until the whey drains away naturally. Use as per the recipe or refrigerate for later use.
- Packaged paneer is easily available in Indian supermarkets.

- Let it stand for 2 minutes and drain in a cloth sieve / muslin cloth over a colander. Discard the whey.

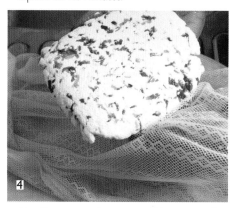

- Place the hung paneer on a flat surface. Fold the cloth over the masala paneer, molding into a square. Place a light weight over the square for 20 minutes.

- Gently unwrap the square. Use as per the recipe or refrigerate for later use.

SAUTÉING PANEER

- Heat 2 tsp oil in a nonstick pan for 30 seconds and gently add the paneer slabs. Fry on moderate heat until light golden brown on both sides.

- Remove and cut into cubes. Use as per the recipe.

MAKING FRESH COOKING PASTES

GINGER (makes 2 tsp)

I

• Place 2 tsp chopped ginger in a mortar.

2

• Pound to a fine paste with a pestle.

3

• Use the fresh paste as required.

GREEN CHILI (makes 2 tsp)

I

• Place 2 tsp chopped green chilies in a mortar.

2

• Pound to a fine paste with a pestle.

3

• Use the fresh paste as required.

GARLIC (makes 2 tsp)

I

• Place 16 peeled garlic cloves in a mortar.

2

• Pound to a fine paste with a pestle.

3

• Use the fresh paste as required.

CELERY (makes 2 tsp)

I

- Place 2 tsp chopped celery stalk in a mortar.

2

- Pound to a fine paste with a pestle.

3

- Use the fresh paste as required.

PARSLEY / MINT / CILANTRO (makes 2 tsp)

I

- Place 1½ tbsp chopped parsley / mint / cilantro leaves in a mortar.

2

- Pound to a fine paste with a pestle.

3

- Use the fresh paste as required (picture shows parsley)

TIP

- While ready-made pastes are available, freshly-made pastes lend the best flavor and aroma to the dish.

WORKING WITH VEGETABLES

BOILING GREEN PLANTAINS

1

- Place the plantains in a pressure cooker, adding enough water to cover them. Pressure cook on moderate heat to one whistle and simmer for 4 minutes.

2

- Cool and drain in a colander.

3

- Peel and use as per the recipe.

BOILING POTATOES

1

- Place the potatoes in a pressure cooker, adding enough water to cover them. Pressure cook on moderate heat to one whistle and simmer for 4 minutes.

2

- Cool and drain in a colander.

GRATING POTATOES

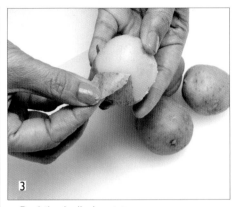

3

- Peel the boiled potatoes.

4

- Grate and use as per the recipe.

TIP

BOILING VEGETABLES WITHOUT A PRESSURE COOKER
- If you don't have a pressure cooker, boil in a conventional pot until tender, increasing the cooking time and adding more water, if necessary.

BOILING LOTUS STEM

- Peel and cut the lotus stem into slanted pieces.

- Place in a pressure cooker, adding enough water to cover the pieces. Pressure cook on moderate heat to one whistle and simmer for 2 minutes.

- Cool and drain in a colander.

BOILING AND CUTTING JACKFRUIT

- Apply oil to your palms and knife.

TIPS

LOTUS STEM

- While buying lotus stems, select the ones with closed ends as the open-ended ones are muddy inside.

JACKFRUIT

- Since unripened jackfruit has a very sticky texture, applying oil on your palms and knife makes handling easier.

- Peel and cut the jackfruit into 1½" pieces.

- Place in a pressure cooker, adding enough water to cover the pieces. Pressure cook on moderate heat to one whistle.

- Cool and drain in a colander.

WORKING WITH VEGETABLES

COCONUT

- Break open the coconut and remove the flesh with a sturdy, sharp knife.

- Peel off the dark brown skin.

- Grate the white flesh and use as per the recipe.

TIPS

COCONUT
- Coconut has a short shelf life; keep it refrigerated and consume within two days.

PEAS
- Adding sugar helps the peas retain their fresh green color.

PEAS

- Heat ½ tbsp oil in a pan for 30 seconds. Add 2 cups / 300 g shelled peas and ¼ tsp sugar. Cook, covered, on low heat until tender, but firm, stirring once.

- Remove and use as per the recipe.

ASPARAGUS

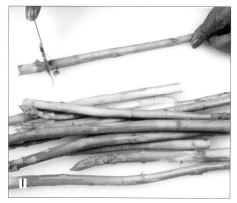

1

- Shave the asparagus spear with a sharp knife or an asparagus peeler.

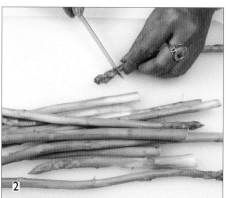

2

- Cut off about 1" of the head (top portion).

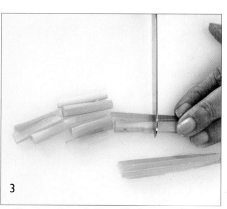

3

- Chop or cut the tender stalks, as per the recipe. Use or discard the hard ends of the spear, as required by the recipe.

CELERY

1

- Using a sharp knife, remove the stringy portions of the celery stalk.

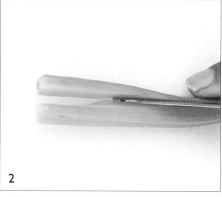

2

- Slice the stalk lengthwise into desired thickness.

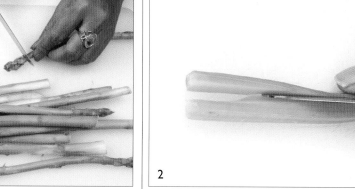

3

- Cut the slit stalk into 1" pieces and use as per the recipe.

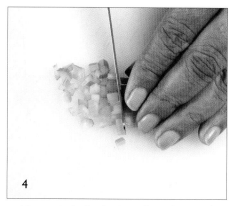

4

- Alternatively, finely chop the celery and use as per the recipe.

TIPS

ASPARAGUS

- Asparagus heads are often used as a garnish.

CELERY

- Celery can have both thick and thin stalks; their thickness does not have a bearing on flavor.
- Celery can be stored, refrigerated in an airtight container, for up to 4-5 days.

COOKING WITH TOMATOES

GRATING TOMATOES

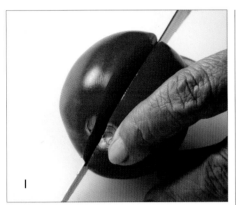

- Halve the tomato lengthwise.

- Grate the tomato, cut-side down until you reach the skin. Use as per the recipe.

ROASTING AND PEELING TOMATOES

- Pierce the head of the tomato with a fork and roast over an open flame until the skin is slightly charred and wrinkled.

- Cool and peel off the skin.

- Cut as per the recipe requirement.

DESEEDING TOMATOES

- Cut the tomato lengthwise into quarters and cut out the seeds with a sharp knife.

- Cut into strips or cubes, or as called for by the recipe.

TIPS
TOMATOES
- Always use firm, plump, red tomatoes.
- Depending on the recipe, the tomato can be deseeded after roasting.

SPECIAL SAUCE PROCESSES

PURÉEING TOMATOES

1

- Cut the tomato into 8 pieces.

2

- Blend to a smooth paste in a blender / food processor

SPICE MIXES

1

- Place the ingredients for the spice mix in a spice grinder / food processor.

2

- Coarsely dry-grind and use as per the recipe.

POPPYSEED PASTE

1

- Soak 2 tsp poppyseeds in ½ cup / 100 ml water for 2 hours. Strain, discarding the water.

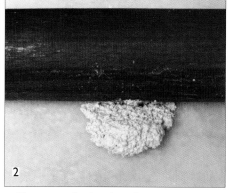

2

- Place on a flat, hard surface and grind to a smooth paste with a rolling pin / stone.

GRATING ONIONS

- Peel the onion and grate.

TIPS

POPPYSEEDS
- Poppyseeds may also be gently dry-toasted, cooled, and then ground in a spice grinder / food processor.
- To obtain poppyseed paste, mix with 1-2 tbsp water.

SPICE MIXES
- Freshly ground spice mixtures evenly impart flavors to the dish and can also help to thicken it.

WORKING WITH SPICES AND SPICE MIXES

TOASTED CUMIN POWDER

- Dry-toast 2 tbsp cumin seeds in a pan on low heat, stirring frequently, until light golden brown.

- Cool and coarsely grind. Store in an airtight container.

GARAM MASALA

- Mix together 2 tbsp black peppercorns, 8 deseeded black cardamom pods, and 2 tsp cloves.

- Grind to a fine powder and store in an airtight jar.

CHAAT MASALA

- Dry-toast 1 tbsp cumin seeds and ¾ tbsp fennel seeds in a pan on low heat, until light golden brown, stirring frequently.

- Cool and grind to a fine powder. Mix with 1 tbsp dried mango powder, 1 tbsp black salt, 1 tsp red chili powder, ½ tsp mint powder, and ¼ tsp ginger powder.

- Store in an airtight jar.

TIP
- Although these spices and spice mixes are available ready-made, the aromas and flavors are best when freshly prepared. Freshly-ground spices may be stored for 2-4 weeks with no significant loss of aroma or potency.

TOASTING SELECT INGREDIENTS

SESAME SEEDS

- Measure 2 tsp sesame seeds into a pan.

- Dry-toast on low heat until light golden brown, stirring continuously; remove.

BULGAR / CRACKED WHEAT

- Heat 1 tsp clarified butter in a wok for 30 seconds; add ¾-1 cup / 125-170 g bulgar / cracked wheat.

- Toast on low heat until evenly light golden brown, stirring frequently; remove.

SEMOLINA

- Place the semolina (as per recipe quantity) in a wok.

- Toast on low heat until evenly browned, stirring frequently, and remove.

PEANUTS

- Heat 2 tbsp oil in a tempering ladle for 30 seconds; add ½ cup peanuts and fry on low heat until light brown, stirring frequently.

- Remove and cool. Skin the peanuts by hand.

TIP
PEANUTS
- You can microwave the peanuts on high for 1-2 minutes instead of frying.

- Coarsely grind, using a mortar and pestle.

WORKING WITH STAPLES

SQUEEZING BREAD

I

- Dip 2-4 slices of bread in 2½ cups / 600 ml water.

2

- Remove immediately and squeeze between your palms.

COOKING RICE

I

- Wash and soak 1 cup / 175 g raw rice in 4 cups / 1 l water for 30 minutes and drain.

2

- Boil 6 cups / 1½ l water and add the soaked rice. Bring to a boil and cook, covered on low heat, until the rice is cooked but still firm.

3

- Drain in a colander and use as per the recipe.

TIPS
RICE

- The cooking time for rice will vary depending on the variety of rice.
- To check if the rice is cooked completely, place a few grains of cooked rice on a plate and press with your index finger to test the texture.
- 1 cup of raw rice will make about 3 cups of cooked rice.

WHILE MAKING DESSERTS

SUGAR SYRUP

1

- Mix 3 tbsp sugar and 2 tbsp water in pan.

2

- Cook gently on low heat, stirring constantly until the sugar dissolves.

3

- Turn off the heat and cool. Use as per the recipe.

LINING AND GREASING

- Line a baking pan with parchment paper and brush the lined base and sides with 1 tsp softened butter.

TIPS

CUT AND FOLD METHOD

- Follow the cut and fold method to mix cake batter, as this technique helps incorporate air into the mixture, making your cake light and fluffy.

POWDERED SUGAR

- Brown sugar can be powdered in the same way as granulated sugar.

POWDERED SUGAR

- If you don't have superfine sugar, grind granulated sugar in a spice grinder or food processor to a fine powder.

CUT AND FOLD METHOD

1

- Use a switched off hand mixer to cut through the batter vertically.

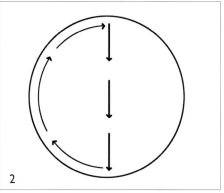

2

- Now move the mixer clockwise from the bottom to the top, in a folding movement. Repeat the action 5-6 times.

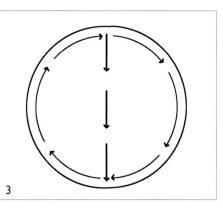

3

- Then turn the electric mixer on and beat for 10 seconds, moving the mixer in a clockwise motion to ensure all the ingredients combine completely.

WORKING WITH NUTS AND DESSERT FLAVORINGS

SLIVERING ALMONDS AND PISTACHIOS

- Finely slice the whole almonds with a sharp knife. Cover and refrigerate. Consume within 7 days.

- Finely slice the whole pistachios with a sharp knife. Cover and refrigerate. Consume within 7 days.

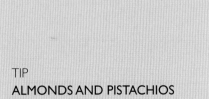

TIP
ALMONDS AND PISTACHIOS
Peeled almonds and pistachios are often used to lend flavor and texture to Indian desserts.

PEELING AND SLIVERING ALMONDS

1

- Soak ½ cup almonds in 1½ cups / 300 ml of water for 8 hours, covered.

2

- Peel the almonds with your fingers.

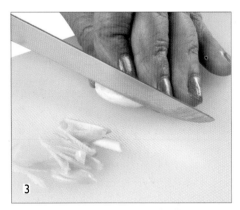

3

- Finely slice with a sharp knife. Cover and refrigerate. Consume within 2 days.

PEELING AND SLIVERING PISTACHIOS

1

- Soak ½ cup pistachios in 1½ cups / 300 ml water for 8 hours, covered.

2

- Peel the pistachios with your fingers.

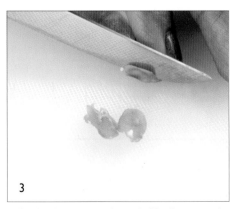

3

- Finely slice with a sharp knife. Cover and refrigerate. Consume within 2 days.

SAFFRON AND GREEN CARDAMOM POWDER

1

- Place the seeds of 8 green cardamom pods in a mortar.

4

- Use quantity indicated in the recipe.

2

- Add ¼ tsp saffron strands.

3

- Pound together to a fine powder with a pestle.

TIPS
SAFFRON AND GREEN CARDAMOM POWDER

- Saffron and cardamom may be pounded individually.
- The powders can also be stored, refrigerated in an airtight container, for up to 15 days.

FRENCH DRESSING
Salad-ras-Francisi

Makes ¼ cup

INGREDIENTS
2 tbsp / 30 ml Olive oil
1 tbsp / 15 ml Balsamic or white wine vinegar (*safed sirka*)
2 tsp / 10 g Powdered sugar (see p. 217)
½ tsp / 2½ g Mustard (*sarson*) powder
¼ tsp Freshly-ground black peppercorns (*sabut kali mirch*)
½ tsp / 2½ g Salt

WITH BALSAMIC VINEGAR

1

- Place the olive oil, Balsamic vinegar, powdered sugar, mustard powder, freshly-ground black pepper, and salt in a mixing bowl.

2

- Whisk well.

WITH WHITE WINE VINEGAR

1

- Place the olive oil, white wine vinegar, powdered sugar, mustard powder, freshly-ground black pepper, and salt in a mixing bowl; whisk well.

TIPS
- Always whisk the dressing well before using. Refrigerate any leftovers and consume within four days
- French dressing can be prepared with either Balsamic or white wine vinegar.

HIGH TEA MENUS

MENU 1

Rose Yogurt Shake (*Lassi Gulbahar*)	21
Indian Burger (*Vada Paav*)	62
Cheese Tikka à la Saffron (*Zafrani Paneer Tikka*)	68
Sautéed Water Chestnuts (*Garma Garam Singhade*)	64
Sesame Milk Fudge Temptation (*Til Khoya Bahaar*)	184
Mint Tea (*Pudina Chai*)	163

MENU 2

Green Breezer (*Angoori Hara Panna*)	25
Savory Bowl 'o' Health (*Daliya Hara Bhara*)	53
Spicy Sweet Corn Patties (*Chatpati Makai Tikkia*, served with Green Coconut Chutney)	55
Nutty Paneer (*Mazeedaar Makai Paneer*)	65
Nutty Calabash Delight (*Lazeez Lauki Lacche*)	190
Mint Tea (*Pudina Chai*)	163

MENU 3

Tender Coco-Berry Refresher (*Strawberry Malaika*)	20
Stuffed Lentil Pancakes (*Bhare Hare Cheele*)	56
Spicy Gram Flour Rolls (*Khandvi*)	60
Lotus Stem Sandwich Fritters (*Kamal Kakdi Sandwich Kurkure*)	74
Gateau Choco-Lait (*Chai-Time Choco Cake*)	196
Mint Tea (*Pudina Chai*)	163

MENU 4

Pomegranate Punch (*Anari Punch*)	24
Savory Bowl 'o' Health (*Daliya Hare Bhara*)	53
Broccoli Cheese Kebabs (*Hare Paneer Kebab*)	70
Stuffed Mushroom Caps (*Khumb Ki Katori*)	78
Date Pineapple Surprise (*Lajawaab Khajoori Ananas*)	182
Mint Tea (*Pudina Chai*)	163

FESTIVE MENUS

Traditionally, celebrations, festivities, and social gatherings in India call for elaborate meals and a variety of dishes. Following drinks and appetizers, guests are invited to partake of curries, lentils, and vegetables, served with rice and breads and an assortment of relishes, yogurts, and salads. The meal is accompanied or followed by dessert. A unique, aromatic finalé with digestive properties signals the end of the meal.

MENU 1

DRINK & APPETIZERS
Pomegranate Punch
(*Anari Punch*) — 24
Cheese Tikka à la Saffron
(*Zafrani Paneer Tikka*) — 68
Stuffed Mushroom Caps
(*Khumb Ki Katori*) — 78

SOUP*
Zucchini Asparagus Fiesta
(*Shatawar Sabz Shorba*) — 30

MAIN COURSE
Black Velvet Lentils
(*Makhmali Dal Makhni*) — 86
Indian Cheese Florentine
(*Saag Paneer Bahaar*) — 92
Cauliflower au Gratin Indien
(*Cheesy Gobi Bake*) — 118
Minty Mushroom Medley
(*Khumb Mattar Mela*) — 114

RICE & BREAD
Hearty Jackfruit Rice 'n' Spice
(*Kacche Kathal Ki Biryani*) — 136
Handkerchief Folds
(*Makhmali Roomali Roti*) — 140

SALAD & YOGURT
Crunchy Oriental Medley
(*Kurkuri Noodle Bhel*) — 42

DESSERTS
Cheesy Cake à la Citron
(*Khushnuma Cheesecake*) — 194
Saffron Fox Nut Pudding
(*Kesari Makhana Kheer*) — 180

MENU 2

DRINK & APPETIZERS
Tender Coco-Berry Refresher
(*Strawberry Malaika*) — 20
Kebab 'o' Lentil
(*Dal Ke Kebab*) — 58
Lotus Stem Sandwich Fritters
(*Kamal Kakri Sandwich Kurkure*) — 74

SOUP*
Potato Cauliflower Pottage
(*Phool Gobi Aloo Shorba*) — 26

MAIN COURSE
Herb 'n' Spice Potatoes
(*Dum Aloo Chaman*) — 96
Spinach Dumplings in Yogurt Sauce
(*Palak Kofta Kadhi*) — 100
Garden Green Peas
(*Hare Bhare Mattar*) — 113
Exotic Vegetable Trio
(*Tirangi Chilgoza Sabzi*) — 117

RICE & BREAD
Water Chestnut & Asparagus Pilaf
(*Singhada Shatwar Pulao*) — 138
Layered Crispy Bread
(*Lachchedaar Tandoori Paratha*) — 142

SALAD & YOGURT
Pasta Mélange
(*Pasta Chaat Salaad*) — 48
Tempered Okra Yogurt
(*Tadkedaar Bhindi Raita*) — 157

DESSERTS
Exotic Lentil Pudding
(*Jashan-e-Moong Halwa*) — 188
Golden Cinnapple Cake
(*Sunhera Apple Cake*) — 198

MENU 3

DRINK & APPETIZERS
Rose Yogurt Shake
(*Lassi Gulbahar*) — 21
Spicy Sweet Corn Patties
(*Chatpati Makai Tikkia*) — 55
Lotus Pearl Kebabs
(*Moti Kamal Kebab*) — 76

SOUP*
Leafy Paneer Soup
(*Pattidar Paneer Shorba*) — 34

MAIN COURSE
Creamy Saffron Paneer
(*Zafrani Paneer Makhni*) — 90
Lentil Nugget Curry
(*Chattpatte Gatte*) — 104
Garden Green Peas
(*Hare Bhare Mattar*) — 113
Petite Potatoes à la Fenugreek
(*Methi Aloo Bahaar*) — 116

RICE & BREAD
Saffron Vegetable Pilaf
(*Zafrani Tahari*) — 132
Layered Crispy Bread
(*Lachchedaar Tandoori Paratha*) — 142

SALAD & YOGURT
Caramelized Pineapple Potato Salad
(*Bhuna Ananas Aloo Salaad*) — 46
Leafy Green Yogurt
(*Bathua Raita*) — 154

DESSERTS
Strawberry Rice Pudding
(*Strawberry Phirni*) — 192
Nutty Calabash Delight
(*Lazeez Lauki Lachche*) — 190

COMMON ACCOMPANIMENTS

Chili Pickle in Minutes
(*Chatpat Achaari Mirch*) — 158
Tangy Root Relish
(*Achaari Kandmool*) — 159

Pickled Onions
(*Pyaz Sirkewale*) — 173
Spicy Tomato Chutney
(*Tikhi Tamatar Chutney*) — 167

Soups are not part of a traditional Indian meal. However, they are often "imported" into the menu at parties and formal occasions.

MENU 4

DRINK & APPETIZERS
Pineapple Kiwi Cooler
(*Ananas Kiwi Sharbat*)   22
Sautéed Water Chestnuts
(*Garma Garam Singhade*)   64
Broccoli Cheese Kebabs
(*Hare Paneer Kebab*)   70

SOUP*
Soup 'o' Mushroom
(*Khumbi Shorba*)   32

MAIN COURSE
Paneer à la Fenugreek
(*Methi Paneer Pasanda*)   84
Spicy Golden Florets
(*Sunhere Rangeele Phool*)   94
Lentil Dumplings in Spicy Sauce
(*Taazi Mangodi Ki Sabzi*)   102
Spicy Green Jackfruit
(*Sukkha Kathal*)   107

RICE & BREAD
Three-Onion Pilaf
(*Pulao Teen Pyaza*)   126
Leafy Fennel Bread
(*Hari Saunfili Roti*)   151

SALAD & YOGURT
Chilled Macbean Delight
(*Sheetal Macrajma Bahaar*)   44
Leafy Green Yogurt
(*Bathua Raita*)   154

DESSERTS
Strawberry Rice Pudding
(*Strawberry Phirni*)   192
Gateau Choco-Lait
(*Chai-Time Choco Cake*)   196

COMMON FINALÈ

Saffron Kahwah (*Kesari Kahwah*)   162
Mint Tea (*Pudina Chai*)   163

MENU 5

DRINK & APPETIZERS
Green Breezer
(*Angoori Hara Panna*)   25
Hint 'o' Mint Cheese Tikka
(*Pudina Paneer Tikka*)   66
Green Floret Fritters
(*Hare Pakode Tilwale*)   72

SOUP*
Green Medley
(*Hariyali Shorba*)   29

MAIN COURSE
Creamy Curried Koftas
(*Kofta Kaju Malai*)   88
Nutty Green Beans
(*Tilwali Phalli*)   106
Tropical Jackfruit Curry
(*Rasedaar Kathal*)   108
Zesty Zucchini Lentils
(*Anokhi Moong Dal*)   110

RICE & BREAD
Tangy Eggplant Pilaf
(*Pulao Baingan Bahaar*)   134
Leafy Fennel Bread
(*Hari Saunfili Roti*)   151

SALAD & YOGURT
Pear 'n' Nut Salad
(*Nashpati Singhara Salaad*)   35
Chili-Garlic Yogurt
(*Tikha-Lehsuni Raita*)   156

DESSERTS
Date Pineapple Surprise
(*Lajawaab Khajoori Ananas*)   182
Cheesy Cake à la Citron
(*Khushnuma Cheesecake*)   194

MENU 6

DRINK & APPETIZERS
Piquant Pear
(*Raseeli Nashpati*)   23
Spicy Gram Flour Rolls
(*Khandvi*)   60
Nutty Paneer
(*Mazeedaar Makai Paneer*)   65

SOUP*
Leafy Mushroom Lentil Soup
(*Lazeez Khumb Dal Shorba*)   28

MAIN COURSE
Curried Golden Dumplings
(*Kofte Kacche Kele Ke*)   82
Smokey Peppers 'n' Paneer
(*Paneer Bhari Shimla Mirch*)   98
Spiced Leafy Lentils
(*Chatpata Chana Palak*)   111
Petite Potato à la Fenugreek
(*Methi Aloo Bahar*)   116

RICE & BREAD
Lotus Stem Pilaf
(*Kamal Kakdi Pulao*)   127
Layered Crispy Bread
(*Lachchedaar Tandoori Paratha*)   142

SALAD & YOGURT
Lotus Stem and Pasta Salad
(*Kamal Kakdi Pasta Salaad*)   40
Chili-Garlic Yogurt
(*Tikha-Lehsuni Raita*)   156

DESSERTS
Gateau Choco-Lait
(*Chai-Time Choco Cake*)   196
Creamy Fruit 'n' Nut Delight
(*Angoori Rabadi*)   178

INDEX